HERS, HIS, AND THEIRS

Gordon Morris Bakken,
SERIES EDITOR

EDITORIAL BOARD
Michal Belknap
Richard Griswold del Castillo
Rebecca Mead
Matthew Whitaker

ALSO IN THE SERIES
*Sex, Murder, and the Unwritten Law:
Courting Judicial Mayhem, Texas Style*
Bill Neal

Hers, His, and Theirs

COMMUNITY PROPERTY LAW

IN SPAIN AND EARLY TEXAS

Jean A. Stuntz

TEXAS TECH UNIVERSITY PRESS

Copyright © 2005, 2010 by Jean A. Stuntz
First edition 2005. Second edition (paperback) 2010
All rights reserved. No portion of this book may be reproduced in any form or by any means, including electronic storage and retrieval systems, except by explicit prior written permission of the publisher except for brief passages excerpted for review and critical purposes.

Portions of this book were published in a different format in *Southwestern Historical Quarterly*, April 2000.

This book is typeset in Arrus. The paper used in this book meets the minimum requirements of ANSI/NISO Z39.48-1992 (R1997). ∞

Designed by Mark McGarry

Library of Congress Cataloging-in-Publication Data
Stuntz, Jean A.
  Hers, his, and theirs : community property law in Spain and early Texas / Jean A. Stuntz. — [New ed.].
    p. cm. — (American liberty & justice)
  Includes bibliographical references and index.
  Summary: "Traces, through legal documents and court cases, the roots of Texas community-property law to Castilian law during the Spanish Reconquest. Examines why Spanish community-law developed so differently from elsewhere in Europe, why it survived in Texas, and what it offered that English common law did not"—Provided by publisher.
      ISBN 978-0-89672-717-5 (pbk. : alk. paper) 1. Community property—Texas—History. 2. Community property—Spain—History. 3. Texas—Civilization—Spanish influences. I. Title.
      KFT1297.S78 2010
      346.76404'   p2—dc22   2010014468

10 11 12 13 14 15 16 17 18 / 9 8 7 6 5 4 3 2 1

Texas Tech University Press
Box 41037
Lubbock, Texas 79409-1037 USA
800.832.4042
ttup@ttu.edu
www.ttupress.org

To my family

Contents

	Preface	ix
	Foreword	xi
	Introduction	xxi
1	The Development of Spain and of Castilian Law	1
2	Las Siete Partidas	15
3	Family Law in the Partidas	31
4	The Transfer of Castilian Laws to New Spain	45
5	The Spanish Legal System Arrives in Texas	63
6	Women's Status in Case Law from San Fernando de Béxar	71
7	The Impact of English History on the Development of English Common Law	87
8	The Application of Spanish and English Laws to Anglo-American Settlers in Mexican Texas	109
9	The Creation of the Republic of Texas and Its Legal System	133
10	The State of Texas and Its Legal System	147
	Conclusion	172
	Appendix A: Chronology	175
	Appendix B: Texas Constitution of 1845	179
	Notes	181
	Select Bibliography	197
	Index	207

Preface

JEAN A. STUNTZ DEEPLY RESEARCHED LEGAL DOCUMENTS to reveal why Texas women in the 1840s were "on a far more equal footing regarding property rights than anywhere else in the United States." Simply put, the Mexican legal experience with Spanish law led Texas legislators and judges to maintain women's property rights. To Texans this might seem a given. Legal experience was the stuff of frontier life, and it created a world of equal property rights. Yet looking west from English colonial America, this was extraordinary. When we read *Hers, His, and Theirs*, this outstanding volume provides an explanation as well as an interpretation of the meaning of liberty and property in Texas history.

Women in seventeenth- and eighteenth-century colonial America experienced civil death in marriage. Patriarchy combined with a strong strain of misogyny created a world of property rights for men. Women resorted to equity courts for legal recourse and in Virginia to brabbling for leverage against men's legal status. Not so in Texas. Spanish law gave women rights in property. Further, women could sue and be sued in court. They could testify in judicial proceedings. Women could regain their dowry when their husband died. Property was liberty for women, and with property they demanded respect within the family. Spanish law encouraged the equal division of property so each child had an inheritance, rather than the English practice of passing real property to the eldest son. Spanish law provided for community property. When a couple married, the property acquired during the marriage belonged to the community of husband and wife, not to the husband. Further, a woman maintained her right to separate property brought to the marriage and her management of that property during marriage. Texas was a different and clearly gendered world of liberty grounded in property rights of women.

Professor Stuntz also analyzes behavior on the operational level of law and society. Women granted power of attorney to people who did business for them at a distance. Texas women bought and sold real and personal property on their own account. Spanish law held them accountable for their actions, and the Mexican and later Texas judicial systems held them liable in civil and criminal actions. Women had the capacity to testify at trial. Women made wills and acted as executors of wills. All of these legal rights were little known, particularly for married women, in American colonial society.

This book is a very welcome addition to the American Liberty and Justice series at Texas Tech University Press. It tells a very Texas tale but speaks volumes about American women's rights.

GORDON MORRIS BAKKEN
Fullerton, California

Foreword

THROUGHOUT THE PAST CENTURY AND A HALF, Texas scholars and historians have largely neglected the influence of Hispanic laws and traditions on the rights of women in the crucially important areas of personal and property rights. Jean Stuntz, as both a historian and an attorney, provides an in-depth, pioneering examination of Spanish law on the frontier of colonial Mexico, particularly Spanish colonial Texas in the middle decades of the eighteenth century. Stuntz compares the original Spanish and English laws and proves that most personal property rights that Texas women hold today stem from the early Spanish laws. She uses numerous examples of Spanish-Texas women, many of whom could neither read nor write, who received equitable treatment from the Spanish governors. Spanish women in Texas knew their rights, a knowledge passed down from mother to daughter over the generations, and, as Stuntz proves, many of them demanded that government officials provide them the protection that they knew those rights guaranteed. Those rights for women, uncommon in English laws, were adopted by Texas legislators after Texas gained independence from Mexico and have proved beneficial for women in Texas ever since. This work provides a new understanding of the importance of our Hispanic heritage and shows how the Anglo ideas of male dominance over women gave way to the Hispanic tradition of giving women more equal standing, at least in terms of property rights.

For centuries, going back to the earliest settlements in Texas and the founding of the thirteen colonies in the United States, the Anglo world has been unaware of the debt that women in the southwestern United States owe to their Spanish predecessors. Whether a result of ethnocentricity or simple ignorance of the laws as they existed in the Spanish world, Anglos have never realized that the laws of community property and women's rights had their origins in the history of Spain itself. Beginning with the eighth century, Stuntz traces the growth of the Spanish legal system and documents the level of power given to women as they were encouraged to follow their men and participate in the nine-century reconquest of Spain from the Moors. As Spanish soldiers extended their march to the frontiers of the New World the same laws followed, as did their women, and spread to the Indian and Mestiza women to whom the King had given his protection. These laws not only gave Spanish, Creole, Mestiza, and Indian women the right to own property, to sue and be sued in court, to testify, and to regain their dowry upon the death of their husband, but they also encouraged many women to demand respect, obedience, and power within the family and within the society. When William Madsen suggests that the "Latin wife . . . did not resent her subordinate role nor envy the independence of Anglo women,"[1] he fails to see the tremendous power that these women wielded within the confines of their own families and their business relationships.[2] Spanish laws and culture thus made their way into Texas and left a profound and permanent mark.

The stories of two Hispanic women in Texas during the nineteenth century provide an apt and particularly telling comparison of the Spanish and Anglo views toward women and show how the laws affected their lives. The clash of cultures that resulted when Anglo Americans began pouring into Texas in the early nineteenth century led to a complex mixture of beliefs and realities for individual women across the state despite the fact that they were protected equally by the laws. The following two cases point out those differences and highlight a surprising effect of the mixed culture: class and education had little to do with how women chose to take advantage of their rights, particularly with regard to property and distribution of wealth. The power of these two women stemmed from the men they married—Patricia de la Garza married a Mexican, who appreciated her rights and accorded her what was her due, while Petra Vela married an Anglo, whose worldview came to circumscribe all of Petra's rights except those he chose to grant her.

Because of the traditions surrounding Spanish laws, Patricia de la Garza de León would have believed in her own rights to property and her power within the business world. Patricia was born into the rapidly expanding Escandón settlements of Nuevo Santander in northeastern Mexico during the late 1770s or early 1780s. It is unknown whether Patricia received an education on the still wild northern Mexican frontier, and there has been continuing debate about whether she was able to read or write. There are no known documents with her signature nor have any letters been found, but despite her lack of writing ability she proved to be a smart and confident woman.[3] Patricia received a large dowry for her marriage to Martín de León, who was a Spanish empresario and the founder of Victoria, Texas, with the knowledge that the dowry would, by Spanish law, remain hers throughout her life. On the frontiers, including Nuevo Santander, a dowry often consisted of animals that could be used to start a ranch,[4] and such was the case with Patricia de la Garza, but the truly substantial part of her dowry came from her godfather, Don Angel Pérez of Soto la Marina. From him she received $9,800 pesos in cash, an amount that was almost unheard of on the northern frontier, money she turned over to her husband to found their first ranch in Texas in 1801.

The couple raised ten sons and daughters, and although Doña Patricia and her daughters were expected to respect and obey their husbands, they were never subordinate to their children or their extended kin's children. Her eldest son, Fernando, might become the next patriarch, but he was always expected to obey and respect his mother. The Spanish culture and laws granted power to age and position, not gender, as the basis for hierarchical obligations.

Upon her husband's death from cholera in 1834, she demanded the return of her dowry by claiming the family's 20,000 acre ranch, and when the family fled to Louisiana to escape the ravages of the Texas Revolution and the unsettled years of the Texas Republic, she sold land in New Orleans and invested the money in mortgages in Louisiana and on her property in downtown Victoria, Texas.[5]

When she returned in 1845, the State of Texas had begun to adopt the Spanish laws and property rights that Doña Patricia knew well. She was able to bring suit in court when two Anglos refused to pay the mortgage money they owed for purchasing her property on the town square in Victoria, and she won. But an even better example of her power over her financial affairs is Doña Patricia's will, which highlights the differences between the Spanish and the Anglo worldviews.

In 1850, as part of her will, she listed all of the money that her children had received from her throughout her life.⁶ She then forgave those debts for her daughters and her male in-laws, leaving "to José María Carbajal the $6,000 he owes me and to Miguel Aldrete the $1000 he owes me." To her eldest son, Fernando, however, she left nothing and bequeathed "to each of my children [except Fernando] equal portions of the $1000 that Fernando borrowed from me to pay debts."⁷ Little is known about Fernando, but he may have joined the Presbyterian church and accepted Anglo culture. Doña Patricia clearly refused to forgive him for his transgressions, whatever they may have been.⁸

Unlike the primogeniture laws, which kept land together under the eldest son and were prevalent in the United States, Spanish partible inheritance laws encouraged equal division of land so that each child would receive an *"herencia,"* or inheritance. In addition to forgiving their debts, Doña Patricia followed this practice and left cattle and mortgages to her two widowed daughters, perhaps now well aware that the Anglo world would be harder for her daughters than the Spanish world had been.⁹

More important than the goods she left them when she died in 1850, were the Spanish beliefs in the rights of women to own property and bring suit that she passed to her children. The Spanish laws and the cultural beliefs they had grown up with gave Patricia's daughters the self confidence to bring suit in the Texas courts to reclaim ranchlands appropriated by Anglo claim jumpers, lawsuits which they won.

Petra Vela, the second of our examples, was born in 1823 in Mier, Tamaulipas, a Mexican river town, two years after Mexican independence from Spain. Her father, José Gregorio Vela may have been a government official in northern Mexico, and he had received a *porción,* or portion, of land on the north side of the Rio Grande from the Mexican government sometime prior to 1821.

Sometime after 1838, Petra, then about fifteen, met Luis Vidal, a lieutenant in the Mexican military. Within two years, census records show that she and Vidal had settled in Matamoros and that she had given birth to her first two children, although there is no evidence of a marriage certificate. With the threat of further invasions from the United States in 1846, Luis Vidal retired from the military, left Petra and her small family, and returned to southern Mexico where he married Manuela Andrade y Castellanos. Petra, now with six children, moved back to Mier, and then, to avoid the American troops, to Monterrey and then further west to Durango. Evidently Luis continued to visit his northern family, because Petra gave birth to Adrian, their only son, in Monterrey and a daughter, Concepción, two years later in Durango.

After the Mexican-American war, Petra returned to Mier, as indicated by the 1849 census records. She is listed as 26 years old with eight children: Luisa 10, Vidal 9, Juana 8, Luis 6, Rosa 5, Adrian 3, Vincenta 1, and Concepcion a newborn. By 1850 Petra, perhaps unaware of the death of Luis Vidal in Veracruz during that year, moved across the border into the United States.

It is unknown how Petra Vela met Mifflin Kenedy, a Pennsylvania-Quaker businessman and entrepreneur who had moved to South Texas and profited from the American invasion of Mexico. Although there is no proof, Petra may have gone to work for Kenedy as his housekeeper. The couple produced a son, Tom, in 1852 and were married two years later. Kenedy did not adopt Petra's children from her relationship with Vidal, and census records indicate that those children lived in a separate house.

The marriage between Petra and Mifflin lasted for thirty years and produced six more children. In 1855 their second son, James, was born, followed by a daughter in 1857, Sara Josephine, or Sarita, John Gregorio in 1858, and then William, or "Willie," the following year. Two years later, Petra gave birth to Phoebe Ann, but the infant died within ten months.

Texas had begun to adopt the Spanish laws of community property, but it was not a view shared by Kenedy. Unlike Patricia de León, who had lived off of her mortgages, Petra depended on Mifflin for money. As a good Catholic, Petra asked her Quaker husband to buy bells, decorations, and stained glass windows for the churches in Brownsville, which he allowed. Later Petra did the same for St. Patrick's Cathedral in Corpus Christi, to which the Kenedys contributed three bells, an organ, and the fresco that graced the walls and ceiling of the beautiful building. Petra also asked for and received dowries to ensure good marriages for her Mexican daughters. In 1856 Rosa married Joseph L. Putegnat in Brownsville and Louisa wed Robert Dalzell, and in 1860 Concepción married Manuel Rodriguez, the mayor of Laredo. Maria Vicenta, during the Civil War, married Frederick Edward Starck, a Union post adjutant at Fort Brown.

By 1865, Kenedy, having profited from the Civil War, invested his money in cattle ranches in South Texas where he built Los Laureles Ranch and, later, La Parra. Petra occasionally joined him, driving up from Brownsville in the family coach. By the 1870s, Petra convinced Mifflin that they should move to Corpus Christi and build a home there. Kenedy built a palatial mansion on a bluff overlooking the bay for her, but Petra, already diagnosed with uterine cancer, did not get to enjoy the lovely home for more than a year. Her daughters, Rosa and Concepción, moved in to care for her.

Petra died in 1885, never having written a will to protect her children as Patricia de la Garza had done. By English tradition, married women were not expected to own anything in their own names, and since everything Petra owned belonged to Mifflin Kenedy, by then several times a millionaire, she could do little but beg him to see to the well being of her children. By August of that year, within six months of Petra's death, Kenedy had bought out all of her Mexican children for $5000 each and removed them as heirs of the ranch. He also cut out his eldest son, Thomas Kenedy, and his daughter, Sara Spohn.

Patricia de la Garza de León, sure of her Spanish legal rights, demanded her inheritance from her husband and left the money and property to nearly all of her children. Petra Vela Kenedy, caught between the two cultures, received nothing from her husband, and neither produced a will nor left property to her children.

The Spanish legal tradition has given women rights, respect, and property in a worldview that, fortunately, the legislators of Texas adopted into our modern legal system. By reviewing the historical basis for our modern laws, both in Spain and in England, Jean Stuntz has provided a new appreciation for the rights of women and the importance of the Spanish influence on our culture.

CAROLINE CASTILLO CRIMM
Sam Houston State University 2005

Notes

1. William Maden, *Mexican Americans of South Texas* (New York: Holt, Rinehart and Winston, 1964), 19.
2. Elizabeth Anne Kuznesof, "The History of the Family in Latin America: A Critique of Recent Work," *Latin American Research Review*, 24:2, (1989), 176–180.
3. Asunción Lavrin and Edith Couturier, "Dowries and Wills: A View of Women's Socioeconomic Role in Colonial Guadalajara and Puebla, 1640–1790," *Hispanic American Historical Review*, 59:2 (May, 1979), 293.
4. Ibid.
5. Inventory of goods of Patricia de la Garza signed at Presas del Rey, January 1, 1801, Vol. 1, p. 34, Index to Deed Records, Victoria County Clerk's Office, Victoria County Courthouse, Victoria, Texas; Arthur B. J. Hammett, *The Empresario: Don Martin de Leon: The Richest Man in Texas*, (Kerville, TX: Braswell, 1971), 8–9, 20–25; Manuel Barrera, *Then the Gringos Came: The Story of Martín de León and the Texas Revolution*, (Laredo, TX: Barrera Publications, 1992), 10–11; Victor M. Rose, *Some Historical Facts in Regard to the Settlement of Victoria, Texas: Its Progress and Present Status*, (Laredo, TX: Daily Times Print, 1883, Reprinted as *Victor Rose's History of Victoria*, Ed. J. W. Petty Jr. (Victoria, TX: Book Mart, 1961), 104–105; William H. Oberste, *Texas Irish Empresarios and Their Colonies*, 2nd edition (Austin: Von Boeckmann-Jones, 1973), 68; Patricia de la Garza to P. B. Cocke, Deed, Volume 1, p. 34, January 24, 1837, Index to Deed Records, Victoria County Clerk's Office, Victoria County Courthouse, Victoria, Texas; Lavrin and Couturier, "Dowries and Wills," 288–295.
6. Ibid.
7. Probate Records, Will of Patricio [sic] Garza de León, October 17, 1850, Vol. 2, p. 591, Victoria County Clerk's Office, Victoria, TX.
8. Will of Patricia de la Garza de León.
9. Ibid.; Gilbert G. González and Raúl Fernández, "Chicano History: Transcending Cultural Models," *Pacific Historical Review* 63:4 (November 1994), 480–48.

Introduction

IN THE MID-1700S, in the tiny villa of San Fernando de Béxar, on the northern fringes of the Spanish empire in North America, Hispanic women had legal rights that would have astonished their British counterparts half a continent to the east. Under Spanish law, even in the sparsely settled land that would one day become Texas, married women could own property in their own names. They could control and manage not only their own property but even that of their husbands. And if their property rights were infringed, they could seek redress in the courts.

While these rights may not seem so incredible to modern readers, to lawyers and historians used to the English common law that gave rise to most American legal traditions they are remarkable for their difference from the English rules. Something so different from the norm raises many questions. Why did the Spanish legal system develop so differently from any other European system? Why did it survive in Texas even after settlement by Anglos in the 1830s? What did this system of community property offer that English common law did not? Why has this aspect of married women's property rights been left out of most books on the subject?

To answer the last question first, Anglocentrism played a large role in the writing of United States histories until the last part of the twentieth century. Ever since Herbert Eugene Bolton created the field of Spanish Borderlands in the early twentieth century, Borderlands historians have been fighting to correct a prejudice they call the Black Legend. This legend is the idea, created by the English during the imperial era and compounded by Anglocentric U.S. historians afterward, that "Spaniards were unusually cruel, avaricious, treacherous, fanatical, superstitious, cowardly, decadent, indolent, and authoritarian."[1] As nineteenth-century Anglo-Americans came into contact with the Hispanics living in what is today Texas and the American Southwest, they carried this prejudice with them. Almost universally, those Anglos were determined to displace despised Hispanic customs with revered English ones. Until the last few decades of the twentieth century, American historians continued to ignore Hispanic contributions to American history, focusing instead on English colonies, English customs, and the English legal system.

A few parts of the Spanish legal system, however, survived in Texas and spread from there to other parts of the United States. In order to understand why that happened, one must first understand why those practices developed and why they were considered so suitable for the frontier. Therefore, this book will open with a short recounting of Spanish history, to show how that nation developed and how the legal system grew along with it. This will be contrasted with English history and a brief look at how the English common law came into existence. Both countries created empires and used their own laws to govern those empires, so this book will contrast the experiences of women in the Spanish and British colonies of North America.

Finally, these two legal systems came together in Texas in the 1830s and 1840s. Why did Hispano-phobic Anglo-American legislators in Texas find the Spanish system so well suited to frontier life that they discarded the English common law they were used to? Why did they adopt community property as the rule of the land? How did the community property laws survive and become part of Texas law? What motivated those men to give and then to protect women's legal rights?

The many legal disabilities of married women under English common law have been written about extensively. *Women and the Law of Property in Early America* by Marylynn Salmon (Chapel Hill: University of North Carolina Press, 1986) skillfully examines how the law was used as a form of social control in America from 1750 to 1830. After the 1830s, many states attempted to use equity courts to establish more just rules for married women and widows, but these rulings were expensive to obtain and did not set precedents for later cases. In Texas, lawyers and judges used Spanish community property laws to establish fairness for women. Because this system was easier to use and more equitable to all concerned, it spread to a few other states. Most states, however, being unfamiliar with the Spanish system and perhaps being prejudiced against anything Spanish, continued to follow English common law.

Because there are so many types of law and so many diverse legal systems, perhaps an explanation of what will and will not be covered is in order. What this work will cover is the development of Castilian laws that became the traditional and customary law of New Spain, including Texas. What this work will not cover is the canon (church) law that governed the legality of marriage and some aspects of family life. The legality of marriages is not at issue here, just property rights within the marriage. Because the focus of the work is to look at why Texas adopted the Spanish system of community property, church law is not applicable. Judicial figures in Spanish Texas, and later the Republic of Texas, did not apply canon law, only the Castilian law of the *Siete Partidas,* which had become the traditional law of New Spain. Other legal systems of continental Europe will not be examined here either, as they do not apply to the question of how community property became the law of the state of Texas.

In addition, this book will not look closely at family life outside what was documented in court cases. The object here is to look at laws as emblematic of social ideals and to look at enforcement of those laws as reflecting judicial recognition of reality. *Homesteads Ungovernable: Families, Sex, Race, and the Law in Frontier Texas, 1823–1860* by Mark M. Carroll (Austin: University of Texas Press, 2001) does an excellent job of describing the harsh realities of domestic life in early Texas. Neither is the administrative framework to be documented here. Readers wishing to know more about the powers and responsibilities of the many officials in the Spanish Borderlands should look at Charles Cutter's superb *The Legal Culture of Northern New Spain, 1700–1810* (Albuquerque: University of New Mexico Press, 1995).

The author wishes to acknowledge the financial support of the Hatton W. Sumners Foundation, the James Bonham Chapter of the Daughters of the Texas Revolution, and the Miss Ima Hogg Graduate Student Scholarship Fund. Gratitude should also be expressed to the Department of History at the University of North Texas for their travel grants and teaching fellowships that allowed her to complete this work and to West Texas A&M University for providing the research time and equipment to get it published. Joseph W. McKnight, professor at the Southern Methodist University School of Law, was very helpful from the beginning of this project. The Borderlands historians who meet annually at the Texas State Historical Association offered guidance and motivation. The staff at the Center for American History at the University of Texas at Austin were incredibly helpful, as everyone said they would be. The Texas Tech University Press staff, especially Judith Keeling, helped get this book through the arduous publication process, and their readers made many good suggestions. The largest debt of gratitude is to Donald E. Chipman, without whom none of this would have happened.

HERS, HIS, AND THEIRS

★ 1 ★

The Development of Spain and of Castilian Law

THE RECORDED HISTORY of Spain begins with the invasion by Romans in 197 B.C.E. It took two hundred years for the invaders to subdue the native inhabitants completely. Then followed four hundred years of peace known as the Pax Romana. The centuries of Roman rule left an obvious physical impact on the Iberian Peninsula. Roman roads and aqueducts and a landholding system known as *latifundia,* whereby some nobles owned vast tracts of land, are notable legacies of Roman rule. The Roman Empire had already begun to disintegrate when the Visigoths swept through Spain and established their capital at Toledo in 554 of the current era. Unlike the Romans, the Visigoths did not leave many tangible reminders of their presence, but their system of laws had a great impact on the future of women in Spain.

The Visigothic Code, *Forum Judicum,* consisted of both ancient laws and laws enacted by various Visigothic kings. It explicitly stated the rights and responsibilities of women. It detailed what constituted a valid marriage, the punishment that awaited a rapist, and most important for this study, the property rights of women. Book Four of the code covered the areas of inheritance and property ownership. Title Two in that book concerned the laws of inheritance, and the first law of that title was that daughters inherited equally with sons. Laws nine and ten reiterated the rights of women in various degrees of affinity to the deceased to inherit equally with men in the same degree of affinity.[1]

Laws of property ownership show how each society defines different levels of privileges, such as whether any particular class of people have the right to own property. Visigothic law, by allowing women the right to own property equally with men, allowed them almost equal citizenship with men. This privilege became more unusual through the centuries as other countries in Western Europe denied property rights to women.

The Iberian Peninsula in Roman times.

The Development of Spain and of Castilian Law 3

In 711, Muslims invaded Spain, conquering in only seven years what had taken the Romans two centuries to accomplish. However, these invaders had the advantage of using all the achievements of the Romans and Visigoths: roads, bridges, and a centralized government. They also had the advantage of a disorganized opponent, the Visigothic king Roderic having disappeared in one of the earliest battles. The victor in that battle was Tariq ibn Ziyad, who named the rock where he landed on the Iberian Peninsula after himself, Gibel al Tariq, now known as the Rock of Gibraltar.[2]

The Moors continued their advance through Spain, conquering all of the territory except for the tiny kingdom of Navarre. Their expansion stopped only when it met the determined forces of Charles Martel at the battle of Tours in October 732. By 740 the Muslim armies had been pushed back south of the Pyrenees. Spain and Portugal are, therefore, the only Western European countries to be occupied for substantial lengths of time by a non-Christian, non-Western culture. Although the Moorish influence is now seen as mostly beneficial with regard to education, religious tolerance, and medicine, the Spanish Christians were determined to take back their country. This crusade, called the *Reconquista*, or Reconquest, was the most influential event in shaping the society of Spain and later that of New Spain (Colonial Mexico).[3]

Chaotic political conditions occasioned by Muslim rulers quarreling among themselves allowed Christians to begin the process of winning back what they considered to be their country. Alfonso III, the Great, was the Christian king of Asturia in the northern part of the Iberian Peninsula from 866 to 910. Alfonso III was both a good military leader and a master of instigating rebellion within the Muslim elite. After the battle of

Polvaria in 878, he won a truce with Muhammad I, who was primarily concerned with putting down internal rebellions that challenged his rule. Alfonso III thus established a stronghold for Christian Spaniards from which to carry out the Reconquest.[4]

The strength of the Christian forces and the rivalry between the Muslims at the beginning of the tenth century seemed to foretell a quick victory for the former, but this was not to be. The Christians were just as divided as the Muslims and could not take full advantage of their triumphs. By 1035 the Reconquest was again stalemated.[5]

In the eleventh century, the Christian kingdoms of Spain changed and grew. As more European influence came into northern Spain, the kingdoms of Castile and Aragon slowly

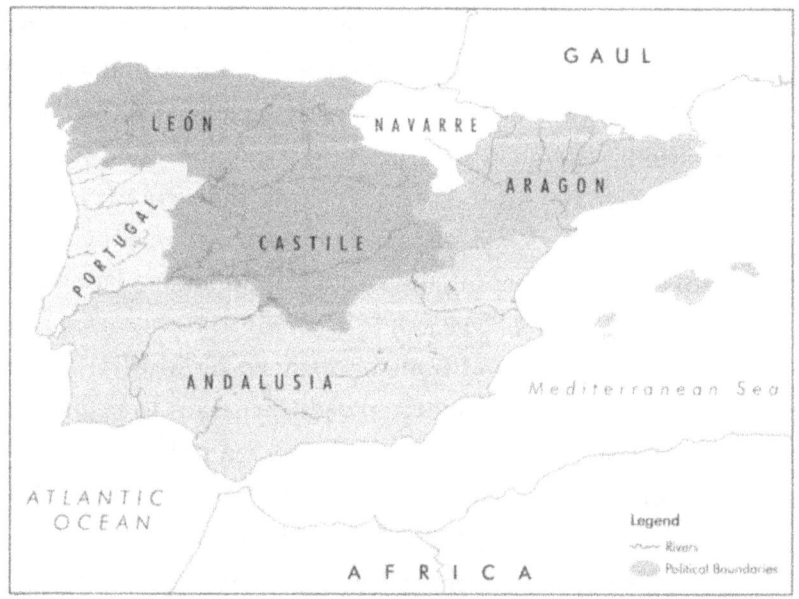

The Iberian Peninsula in the middle of the Reconquest, circa 1150.

emerged. These two kingdoms would quickly overshadow the older kingdoms of León and Navarre and become preeminent in the Reconquest. The kingdom of Castile in particular adapted to the needs of frontier warfare and provided the driving force that would eventually reunify Spain under Christian rule. Castile's responses to the exigencies of the Reconquest became apparent as it conquered more and more territory. The various rulers proclaimed changes in laws to ensure the spread of Christian civilization in newly conquered territory. For two centuries the Christians and Muslims fought each other and themselves, resulting in many impermanent changes and an overall balance of power.[6]

The period from 1212 to 1369 encompassed the most productive part of the Reconquest, whereby Christians recaptured almost all of the Iberian Peninsula. The battle of Las Navas de Tolosa (1212) was a great defeat for the Muslims, and for the next century and a half they were divided by conspiracies, rebellions, and civil wars. As Christians reconquered Spain, they established and solidified their kingdoms. Castile expanded greatly as its rulers conquered most of the remaining Muslim territory. By the end of this era, the Muslims controlled only the kingdom of Granada, and Castile was the most powerful of the Christian kingdoms. Aragon, because of its ties with France and its expansion abroad into the Italian peninsula, was the second most powerful kingdom within Spain.[7]

This era also saw important changes in government. As new areas came under Christian control, local governments became important as a means of settling the conquered lands. The local council, or *cortes*, emerged as a powerful parliamentary assembly. Representatives from the three estates—prelates, nobles, and townsmen—came together when summoned by the king.

The most important function of the *cortes* was to consent to the king's taxation, but it also had a growing role in internal administration and foreign relations. Power over the king's purse strings gave parliamentary members the ability to safeguard their own rights and privileges, and even to expand them.[8]

Towns, more so in Castile than in the other kingdoms, remained relatively autonomous. Aristocrats ruled each town and did not want to give up any of their power to the king, nor did the townspeople wish to surrender any of their power to a monarch. Even popular and respected kings would be challenged when they infringed on traditional rights of nobles or towns. Alfonso X, widely respected as a man of intelligence, discovered this attitude when he tried to regularize the laws of Castile. He ordered that royal laws be written and distributed so that all Castilians would know their rights, but the nobles resisted to the point of removing Alfonso from the throne. Alfonso X's *Fuero Real* encountered such great resistance because the king was trying to make laws equally applicable to all citizens instead of favoring the nobility. The same aristocrats were usually members of the *cortes* and so had a direct voice in opposition to the expansion of royal power. Castilian men also banded together in informal brotherhood associations, or *hermandades,* to defend their mutual interests. All of these actions allowed Castilian cities more freedom in enacting their own codes, many of which increased the rights of women, as discussed below.[9]

The last phase of the Reconquest began in 1469 with the marriage of Ferdinand of Aragon to Isabella of Castile. How the marriage came about illustrates several aspects of Spanish society during these years. Ferdinand was prince of Aragon and king of Sicily. In 1469 he was seventeen years old and seemingly embodied everything desirable in a prince. He had been raised during a period of almost perpetual warfare waged by his father, King Juan II. Ferdinand was skilled in the art of war, educated as befitted his station, and singularly charming in person. He was diplomatic, devious, and disarming. At the time of his marriage, he had fathered two children out of wedlock. All noble fathers in Europe who knew Ferdinand seemed to want him to marry their daughters. Within Spain, especially, rival factions wanted a marital alliance with the prince of Aragon.[10]

Isabella's role was much more complicated, and she had to be both devious and determined to accomplish her goal of marrying Ferdinand. Her half-brother, Henry IV, had ruled Castile from 1454 to 1467. Henry was not a popular figure in Castile: he discarded too many traditions, was too peace-loving and licentious, and, worst of all, he had no heir. His insubordinate nobility, in order to further discredit him, spread rumors that he was homosexual, impotent, and irreligious. Historians are in disagreement on whether these accusations were true. Regardless, that his nobles spread these rumors and accepted them as truth shows how little they respected their king. Henry's alleged daughter by Juana of Portugal was commonly assumed to be the daughter of Beltrán de la Cueva, the powerful duke of Alburquerque; and so widespread was this belief that the daughter was called Juana "la Beltraneja." The Castilian nobility took advantage of the lack of leadership and started a civil war aimed at promoting Isabella's younger brother Alfonso as king. Isabella was caught in the middle, with nobles on both sides wanting her to join them. She finally gave her support to her teenage brother when he and his nobles gave their pledge to let her marry as she wished.[11]

Young Alfonso died suddenly and mysteriously in early July of 1468—allegedly as a result of eating a spoiled trout. Rumors abounded, however, that he had been poisoned by Juan Pacheco, Marqués de Villena, who wanted to start his own dynasty. Pacheco had worked hard to convince Alfonso to force Isabella to marry a prince from either Portugal or France. He planned to have his own daughter marry either Ferdinand of Aragon or Alfonso of Castile, whichever became more powerful. When Alfonso proved to be resistant to Pacheco's plans, Ferdinand appeared a better candidate for his daughter. Pacheco then planned to have Isabella marry the elderly King Alfonso of Portugal. The potential marriage of the princess of Castile to the king of Portugal would bring the two kingdoms together again. Isabella kept her own counsel through these years but politely refused to marry anyone.[12]

With young Alfonso dead, the dissident faction tried to get Isabella to declare herself queen and continue the war against Henry, but she refused to do so. Instead, she wrote to the king and declared herself his heir presumptive. This was a wise choice on her part, because Spanish society was not likely to accept an unmarried queen as sole ruler. Henry and the rebels reconciled, and Isabella's marriage became the subject of a power struggle between Pacheco and Alfonso Carrillo de Acuña, archbishop of Toledo. Carrillo was instrumental in bringing together Isabella and her choice of husband, Ferdinand, prince of Aragon and king of Sicily.[13]

The marriage itself could have been the subject of a romantic novel instead of the grimly serious matter of joining two kingdoms. Isabella had to act surreptitiously because Henry was still determined to have her marry the Portuguese king. With the connivance of Carrillo, Isabella sent letters to Ferdinand to find out if he would be willing to join their kingdoms by matrimony. He was agreeable, and once he had sent her a

The Development of Spain and of Castilian Law 9

gold and ruby necklace as a pledge of his intent, the couple secretly made plans to marry. More letters sent secretly arranged their first meeting. In the middle of the night of October 14, 1469, Ferdinand arrived in Valladolid to meet Isabella. He had traveled in disguise, acting as servant to his retainers. She was eighteen, plump, and pretty, with auburn hair and blue-green eyes. He was seventeen, of medium height with dark brown hair and a charming smile. It was apparently love at first sight, a love that would last a lifetime. They talked for hours that first night and made formal promises to wed. Ferdinand left while it was still dark, only to arrive as himself a few days later. Castilians enthusiastically supported Ferdinand as the best husband for Isabella, and the couple wed.[14]

The importance of that wedding, for the purposes of this work, lies in the marriage contract that Isabella had Ferdinand sign. Castile was a larger, more prominent, and richer kingdom than Aragon, and Isabella was determined to keep all her royal prerogatives intact. She insisted that Ferdinand swear to obey the laws and customs of Castile, to live in Castile, and not to leave the kingdom without her knowledge. They would sign all decrees jointly and share all titles equally. Ferdinand was a bit hesitant to accept Isabella as an equal, but she promised to appear in public as though she were ruled by him. She kept her promise. In all their years together, Isabella always appeared to obey Ferdinand's decisions, and she insisted that he sign all documents first, so that he appeared more powerful. Behind the scenes, though, Isabella would use all her wiles to persuade Ferdinand to her way of thinking, and she usually got her way. Because of their contract, and the way they followed it, Castilian laws and customs became the laws and customs of all Spanish territory in the New World.[15]

The joining of the two most powerful kingdoms of Spain, and their mutual desire to have all of Spain be as one nation, one Crown, and one faith, led to the final defeat of Muslim Granada, and later, the expulsion of Jews from Spain. Ferdinand led the armies of Castile and Aragon against the last Muslim kingdom of Granada, which fell January 2, 1492. The Reconquest was over.[16]

Several aspects of the centuries-long struggle had great consequences for Spanish society. The Reconquest was not the work of a national army, nor was it led by a single king. Individuals led campaigns, and they became wealthy through the booty and land acquired. Good warriors became great captains, and great captains became high nobles. The aristocracy was the military elite, and they held all military power. Another important con-

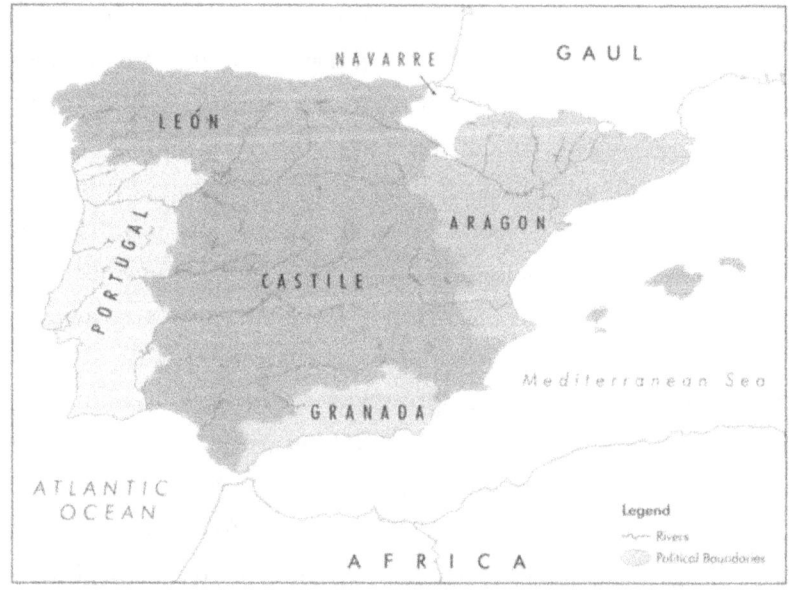

Spain at the end of the Reconquest, 1492.

sideration was the goal of spreading Christianity, the ostensible motivation for the Reconquest. This linkage of warfare and religion carried over into the conquest of the New World.

From the Reconquest came the idea that income derived from conquest, not work. Gentlemen did not work for material gain but enjoyed wealth as a result of plundering from the infidel. And on the frontier, the only occupations that were suitable for nobility were fighting and stock raising, because aristocratic military captains kept herds of livestock on the frontier to feed their men. Thus, ranching became linked with the aristocracy. Ranching, like warfare, was conducted on horseback, and it became one of the few professions suitable for a gentleman. At the same time, the aristocracy gained great political power because of their private armies. As mentioned, they did not fight under the king, nor for him. They fought for themselves and for their own private gain. These attitudes transferred easily to the conquest of the New World in the sixteenth and seventeenth centuries.[17]

Farming, on the other hand, became the lot of peasants. For those aristocratic warriors, land could lead to wealth, but it was not the object of their ambition. Power and glory came from warfare, not from owning land. Other European countries tended to value land itself as the measure of wealth. Their laws, therefore, tended to protect property rights, as opposed to Castilian laws aimed at protecting the community.

A further innovation was the growth of towns. Since it was too dangerous for people to live alone on the frontier between Muslims and Christians, the latter especially banded together and formed villages. Whenever one side won a village from the other, the victors would encourage their own people to immigrate to that settlement in order to repopulate it and hold it against the enemy. Communities developed as the frontier progressed, and each time the frontier progressed, Spanish civilization grew. This spread of Spanish society was an important goal of the Reconquest, and laws would help enforce the Spanish ideas of what constituted civilization.[18]

Throughout the Reconquest, men seized land from other men, but women were needed to settle it and extend the Spanish community to the new land. Newly won cities had to be repopulated with Spanish people as the Moorish population was killed, captured, or forced to convert or move. Women, therefore, were needed as wives of colonizers, mothers of the next generation of defenders, and indispensable members of the new Spanish communities. This spread of Spanish civilization was an intrinsic part of the Reconquest. Not only did the Moors have to be removed from the land, but also Spanish Christians had to move in to replace them. The land could not be considered truly reconquered until Spanish communities controlled the area. To induce people to move to the hazardous new areas, a city would pass *fueros* (codes of laws) that guaranteed property rights and justice under the law. Significantly, to persuade single, respectable women to come to the new territory and marry, and to persuade wives to join their husbands in this dangerous area, the *fueros* protected and even expanded the rights of women.[19]

The *fueros* regarding women encouraged and fostered marriage, birthing children, and settled life in the cities. Many women who lived in the cities were respected as property-owning citizens, and maidens of landowning families had great value as prizes for bachelor warriors whom the citizens wished to have settle in the city. This consideration did not mean that women were completely independent, for they were not. The husband still controlled the wife's property, but community pressures and the wife's family apparently kept him from wasting it. The wife was an important part of the family, and she shared in all the financial gains and losses of the marriage. Since most husbands were absent while fighting in the wars of the Reconquest, it was up to the wife to handle many of the family's everyday responsibilities and financial transactions.[20]

Also, because of sporadic fighting, there were many widows on the Spanish frontier. These women had to honor the memory of their deceased husbands for one year, but after that they were encouraged to remarry. Remarriage helped to repopulate the town, kept the widow from losing her reputation, and placed her once more under the control of a man. According to the mores of that society, all women needed the protection and control of a man, whether father, brother, or husband, and widows did not fit into the pattern. Therefore, there was great incentive and peer pressure for the widow to reenter normal society by remarrying.[21]

Married women filled important and respectable roles in community life, especially when their husbands were absent. They presided over bakeries, bathhouses, washing places at the river, and other traditionally female occupations such as spinning and weaving. If disputes occurred in these areas, women served as witnesses for the lawsuits that resulted. Women also witnessed land sales, arraignments, and other legal matters; and they had to pay taxes if they were the head of household. They could sue and be sued on their own, meaning that their husbands did not have to be parties to the suits, and they were responsible for the actions of their children and servants.[22]

Women, mostly married women and widows, held respectable jobs. They might serve as domestic servants, as wet nurses (who were held in high esteem), or as shopkeepers. Other married women worked alongside their husbands in shops and in various occupations. Widows often kept up their husband's shop or profession after he died, and if they remarried their new husband would have a ready-made career.[23]

All of these examples show that women were an important part of frontier society, necessary to the continuance and expansion of the Spanish community. Their property rights increased as various city councils lured them to settle within the village boundaries. Their increased legal rights were guaranteed by the city codes, and the pioneer women passed these rights on to their daughters and granddaughters. Eventually these expanded rights became traditional, an ingrained part of Castilian culture. Although respectable Castilian women usually were not totally independent of the protection of a man, they had many more legal rights than women in other European societies. Castilian women were not entirely subservient to their men, for women had the right to own property, and this right was the basis for all other civic freedoms.

The legal system ensured that Castilian women would be able to take care of their own rights in the event of widowhood. Women were much too valuable in the effort to repopulate and civilize the newly reconquered areas to be relegated completely to a subservient, helpless position. Since the men were often absent during warfare, women had to be capable of carrying on the family's affairs. This capability spread to other areas of feminine jurisdiction, and females were the equals of males in these areas. It was this ability, this accumulation of rights passed down through generations of Castilian women, that was so important to the settlement of the frontier in the New World.

✷ 2 ✷

Las Siete Partidas

ONE OF THE BENEFITS of the long period of Islamic cultural influence in Spain was the emphasis on learning that filtered into medieval Christian society. The twelfth and thirteenth centuries were the height of cultural transmission of Islamic knowledge to Christian cultures. This is reflected in the many translations into Spanish, especially made by scholars in Toledo, of Islamic versions of ancient works by such people as Galen and Ptolemy. During this time, Spanish kings had more available income derived from land acquired by their own conquests, and they came to enjoy scholarship and the arts. The revival of Roman law made intellectuals aware of the disorganized state of Spanish law, and, as a result, differing regions such as Aragon and Navarre codified their laws. However, the greatest intellectual undertaking of that time was the codification and unification of diverse Castilian law under King Alfonso X (1254–1286).[1]

In 1256 Alfonso X, known as *"el sabio,"* or "the learned," ordered the reorganization of the laws of Castile. The first book of laws, the *Fueros Reales,* or *Royal Laws,* did not cover a wide enough expanse, so Alfonso dictated that a work encompassing the whole of law be compiled. The actual compilers are not known but may have included Alfonso himself. The sources consulted were so vast and the authorities cited so numerous that it took more than ten years for many scholars to complete the task. When finally finished, this compilation proved to be one of the great works in the history of law. It portrayed "a rational system of universal justice under central monarchy and [was] the first great didactic literary classic in the Castilian vernacular."[2]

Las Siete Partidas, or *Seven Divisions of Law,* is so named because it is divided into seven parts. It draws heavily from Roman law, but it also contains canon law, maritime law, Visigothic law, and the customs and *fueros* of the various Spanish cities. It cites both Scripture and the writings of saints as authorities. Though it was written at a time of much Moorish influence, it does not cite many Islamic sources, because of Christian attitudes toward Muslims during the Reconquest.[3]

The *Partidas* covered every known aspect of law, from the role of the king to appropriate candidates for a mistress, with rationale given for each. At that time, the Spanish were exceptionally litigious, as evidenced by the number of lawsuits recorded. Therefore, the compilers of the *Partidas* went into great detail to try to cover every possible contingency. This attempt was also aimed at unifying laws throughout Castile. Each town had its own code of laws, many of which were contradictory, not only with other towns but also within the code itself. The *Partidas* were not intended to supercede these laws, but to give the towns an example that they could copy in rewriting their own laws in the manner of the *Partidas.*[4]

The *Partidas* gave great power and responsibility to a paternalistic, benevolent king. This idea of a unified state was threatening to the nobility of the Iberian Peninsula, who were used to significant autonomy. The various political powers, both the nobility and the townspeople, opposed the concept of a powerful monarch, as expressed in the *Partidas*, because it took away many of their traditional rights. They would eventually use this supposed usurpation as a justification to depose Alfonso. For his part, Alfonso had never intended for this code of laws to become effective immediately as the sole law in the land, for even the king himself saw that it was too visionary for that time. However, he did intend for it eventually to become the law of the land, after people became accustomed to its ideas. That was precisely what happened.[5]

The *Partidas* was written in the newly standardized Castilian vernacular, so schools and universities used its text in teaching grammar and vocabulary for the next three centuries. Since its laws included commentary that explained the philosophy behind each law, it was used in philosophy as well as law classes. Over the years, many of the upper classes went to the universities to obtain their education, and they came to regard the law as expressed in the *Partidas* as the true law. Likewise, men who became the bureaucrats and courtiers read and studied these laws. The ideas contained within the *Partidas* also touched the middle and lower classes: when these people came into legal situations, judges resolved the issues on the basis of these codes. Its precepts thus gradually filtered into the minds of all people. The law presented in the *Partidas* became the traditional law as the people knew it. An examination of the laws that pertained to women provides insight into how Spaniards regarded the role of women in society.[6]

The division of *Las Siete Partidas* into its seven parts is not logical to modern minds. Though seven was used in many cases during the Middle Ages because it was considered a perfect number, the compilers apparently used seven parts of law in order to honor Alfonso: the first letter of the introduction to each section spells out his name.[7] The sequence of these laws also gives insight into medieval Spanish society. The first part deals with canon law, because the Church was paramount, and with laws in general; the second part with government and administration, because the state was second in importance; and the third part with property and maintaining society. These last two areas, property and maintaining society, are usually dealt with separately in modern American jurisprudence, as each covers an enormous amount of case law. The fourth part of the *Partidas* treats domestic relations, and the fifth deals with financial obligations and maritime law. Again, these two areas are usually separated in American jurisprudence, though debts and shipping are still closely linked. The sixth part covers wills and inheritances, and guardianships, and the seventh discusses crime and general principles of law. Again, two separate bodies of law are joined in one part, but perhaps a bit more logically, for the modern mind can readily associate crime with the practice of law.[8]

The main impression a reader receives from the *Partidas* is the extraordinary detail with which each area is covered. As in Roman law, the compilers tried to think of every single possibility for each situation and decide the legal consequences in each case, depending on what had been effective in earlier generations. This approach aimed at providing stability to Castilian society, because everyone would know, through custom and usage, his or her own rights and responsibilities. This understanding was important, for the Castilians were litigious by nature and brought lawsuits instead of settling slights by combat, as in other European societies. Because everyone knew the rules, even royalty had to follow the dictates of law. Neither kings nor emperors could grant royal concessions that were contrary to law, nor could they deprive people of their property without following proper procedure or giving due compensation.[9] This adherence to law by the highest nobility is all the more remarkable when compared to the attitudes of the absolute monarchs of later European countries.

Women were well protected in Castilian society, though their legal status both guarded and limited their actions. The law protected women from conniving and unscrupulous people, as well as from their own presumed feminine weaknesses. For example, a general limitation and protection presumed that women had little contact with the business world. Therefore, they could not be held to their contracts if those contracts turned out to be against their best interests. Exceptions could be made if the woman wanted to be able to do business and proved her ability before a judge. Women's legal rights and responsibilities were carefully delineated in the *Partidas,* and the detailed explanations as to why certain limits applied to women gives the reader a clear view of a woman's place in medieval Castilian society. As noted, the *Partidas* were not arranged in a logical or systematic order. Therefore, various aspects of law regarding women will be discussed in this text not by their arrangement in the actual work but by their modern classification in contemporary American jurisprudence. These classifications are the legal capacity of women: their ability to make contracts, to hold property, and to sue and be sued for civil wrongdoings, their domestic relations, and their liability for criminal actions. The first four topics will be discussed in this chapter, the last two in the following chapter.

In the *Partidas,* women held almost the same legal capacity as men but with several important limitations. For example, though judges usually did not want women to be in their courtroom, women could be, and often were, witnesses to a lawsuit. Their testimony was as fully credible as a man's, but as a protection for her reputation, a woman could not be summoned to make an appearance in court. Instead, the judge himself was required to go to the woman's house to take her deposition, or to send a notary to do it. If a woman was a party to a civil suit, she should send an attorney to represent her instead of appearing in court. The rationale for these rules held that it was not proper for women to mingle publicly with men. However, if the woman was accused in a criminal case, she did have to appear in court.[10]

For similar reasons, a woman could not be an advocate for anyone. Part 3, Title 4, Law 3 of *Las Siete Partidas* reads,

> No woman, however learned she may be, can act as an advocate for others in court. There are two reasons for this; first, because it is neither proper nor honorable for a woman to assume masculine duties, mingling publicly with men... [a]nd, moreover, when women lose their modesty it is a difficult matter to listen to them and dispute with them.[11]

Another reason for restricting circumstances under which women could appear in court is given in the law itself. In ancient times, a woman named Calpurnia was very learned. She would act as an advocate for others and was so learned that the judges could not overcome her arguments, whereby she would prevail over male advocates. This prospect, in a male-dominated society, was so unseemly that the compilers of the *Partidas* acted to prevent such a circumstance from ever happening again.[12]

Although women could never act as advocates for others, under special circumstances they could act as guarantor or surety for others if they wished, although they could not be compelled to do so. A surety is generally defined as a person who stands liable for another's obligations if the primary debtor does not repay the debt. The general rule barred women from acting as sureties for other parties, "for it would not be proper for women to go into court...and be compelled to resort to places where many men are assembled, and to do things which might be contrary to chastity." There were, however, seven exceptions to this rule. These exceptions deal with areas normally associated with women's roles in society and with the circumstances where it could be shown that the woman in question knew what she was doing. A woman could be surety for the amount needed to free a slave. She could be surety for another woman's dowry. If she wished, she could renounce the laws that protected her and become a surety for a man, in which case she would be bound by all the laws that bound men. If she received compensation, this proved that she understood the consequences of her actions, and she could be held liable as a surety. A woman could be surety for her own acts, and for a person from whom she was expected to inherit. Lastly, if she fraudulently dressed like a man and deceived others into thinking she was a man, she could be held liable for her actions. In this circumstance, she would have to pay what she had guaranteed for another, because the protection was given to women not so they could defraud others, "but on account of their artlessness and their natural weakness."[13]

Despite their "artlessness" and "natural weakness," women did have legal power to act for others under specific circumstances. If a widow petitioned the king and officially waived all laws that protected her, she could be named legal guardian for her own children. However, if she remarried, the children had to be taken from her and given to their nearest respectable relative. The rationale given for this is that the widow would have so much affection for her new husband that she would neglect her children, or perhaps even injure them. If she mismanaged her children's property while she was guardian, she could be held liable for it. Another example of a woman's legal capacity to be responsible for others is that, under special circumstances, she could adopt an heir. The general rule was that a woman could not adopt children, since it was assumed that she, if she were of suitable age, would be able to bear her own. But if a woman lost a son in battle, and the king consented, she could adopt another son to replace her loss.[14]

Women of good character could be effective witnesses in legal battles, for their testimony carried the same weight as that of men. One restriction to this law was that a woman could not testify in favor of her husband, but then neither could the husband testify in favor of his wife. (The same is true in English common law.) The same restriction applied to a brother testifying for his brother. This limitation was not, then, actually based on gender, but on relationship. The other exception to a woman's full capacity to act as a witness was gender-based, and this pertained to wills. Women could not be witnesses to a will. However—and this shows the detail with which these laws were drafted—if a person had the physical characteristics of both sexes but was more similar to a man than to a woman, this person could indeed witness a will.[15]

Though judges held enormous power in Castilian society, the rights of women were expressly protected from magistrates by law. Women held a special exemption from being summoned to appear before a judge who wished to marry her without her consent, either to himself or to another. Neither could the judge summon the woman to his chambers to have his way with her, nor to use force of any kind upon her. If this happened, neither she nor any member of her family ever had to appear before that judge, and anyone who wished to make a complaint against her or her family had to take it to a different court. All appeals from widows and orphans went directly to the king, because he was required by law and chivalric codes to protect those who needed him most.[16]

Legal capacity could be lost in various ways. Marriage put many women's legal rights in abeyance for the duration of the marriage. For instance, a married woman could not accuse anyone of a crime, except that of treason, without at least the implied joinder of her husband or guardian. The same restriction applied to minors, persons with a bad reputation or who had been proven to be false accusers, the very poor, and criminals. Treason was again the sole exception, because it was such a serious crime that anyone, even a slave or a married woman, could accuse a person of that offense. In civil cases, likewise, anyone who suspected guardians of mismanaging their ward's property could accuse them and bring them to justice. Mothers, grandmothers, sisters, and nurses, any one of whom could be a married woman, had the obligation to bring such an accusation on behalf of the children.[17]

If a woman lost her good reputation, she lost most of her legal rights. This tradition would be very important in the New World. For example, it was considered improper for a widow to remarry within a year of her husband's death. Such action might cast doubt on the parentage of any children born during her widowhood or soon after the second marriage, and it also might raise suspicion that the widow had killed her first husband in order to marry the second. Such a woman could not inherit from anyone other than her immediate family. As discussed above, any widow, even one of good reputation, lost guardianship of her own children when she remarried. The children might actually remain in her custody, especially if they were less than three years old, but a male relative would be responsible for the protection of the children's property.[18]

The most common way for a woman to lose her reputation was to be involved in an extramarital affair. Even the suspicion of involvement was enough in some cases for the woman to become infamous. "Infamous" was the legal term used to denote people who had lost their good reputation, their credibility, their honor, and their standing in the community. For example, men could become infamous if they fought wild beasts, sang, or jested for money, but not if they performed these entertainments for free. The law listed several ways for a woman to become infamous. A woman who was found in a place where she had committed adultery, or had committed "a wickedness with her body" less than a year after her husband's death, was considered to be infamous. Women who acted as procuresses, or who kept "slaves or free women in her house inducing them to commit wickedness with their bodies for money," were infamous, though they themselves might commit no wickedness personally. Women did not have to charge for their entertainments, as was the case with men, in order to lose their standing in society, but that did remove all doubt as to the state of their reputations.[19]

Certain legal presumptions limited the extent of a woman's rights. When twins were born, one male and one female, the male was presumed to have been born first so that, if applicable, he could inherit exclusively. Since under Castilian law all legitimate children inherited a portion of the parents' estate, this presumption applies only to certain entailed properties. When a husband and wife died in a common accident, such as a shipwreck, the wife was presumed to have died first, because of her being naturally weaker. This cleared the way for the husband's heirs to inherit first. But legal presumptions could act protectively, too. The sons of traitors could not inherit from either parent, because of the legal presumption that they would have been involved in the treason, but daughters could inherit from their mothers, because "no man should presume that women will commit treason."[20]

Married women generally did not make contracts, but they could if they renounced all protective laws in their favor. Widows had little restriction on their power to make contracts. There was an explicit form that defined how a contract should be drawn, and the contract had to have the wife's consent to a sale of either her separate property controlled by the husband, or of community property owned by both spouses. The wife had to verify that she released all her rights to the property and bound herself to abide by the sale made by her husband. There was also a form whereby a man agreed to give his daughter in marriage, guaranteeing the dowry as well as the daughter's consent, but the daughter was not a party to this actual contract. However, a man and a woman could make a contract to marry, and in some cases that sufficed for the formal union. There were also forms for dowries and gifts from wives to husbands, and the wife was bound by the contract.[21]

Women could and did hold property in their own names. The distinction for women was not so much between real and personal property, though there were many laws referring to movables, as between dotal and paraphernal property. Dotal property was that which the wife brought into the marriage, i.e., her dowry. Paraphernal property was all her property not included in the dowry, i.e., her separate property. The law protected her paraphernal property; she would have to give power of attorney to a male relative in order for them to control it. Publicly the husband controlled all the property owned by both, but the wife could, if necessary, legally enjoin him not to waste her portion, and she had to officially consent to all sales of her own or commonly owned property.[22]

The wife could even control the husband's property, though under very limited circumstances. Usually a wife had to have her husband's consent before she could give alms to the poor, go on a pilgrimage, or fast. If she had her own property, however, she could give alms from it and also from any of the husband's property that was normally under the control of women, for example, food in the kitchen. A wife could therefore give bread to the poor, even though it actually belonged to the husband as long as it was a reasonable amount. (Lawyers through the ages have made a lot of money arguing over what is reasonable.) If she saw a poor person and thought that her husband would want to give him some money, she could do that, too, though she was not obligated to do so if she thought her husband would beat her for doing it. Lastly, if she saw a person in such straits that if he or she were not given alms immediately that person would die, she could give alms out of her husband's property, even if he had strictly forbidden it.[23]

The compilers of the *Partidas,* at the prompting of their

monarch, showed their concern for women's property rights by including several protections for women and their property. A married woman could not usually lose her property through abandonment, because the husband was presumed to be in control and his lack of judgment should not prejudice her rights. If, however, the property was part of her dowry and the marriage was dissolved, then she would be in control of her own property and could lose it through abandoning it for a long enough period of time. Also, if her husband was an obvious spendthrift and she did not go to court to demand the return of her dowry, then she was held to have acquiesced in its loss and could not later regain the property.[24]

The only bar to a woman inheriting was a poor reputation, and even then she could inherit from her immediate family. After the husband died and before his estate was distributed, the dowry of the wife was repaid to her, for it was not considered part of the husband's property. When a rich man married a poor woman, she could receive one quarter of his estate as her share, but not if she owned enough property to support herself.[25]

Sometimes the reasons for the protection of women are obvious in the laws, as when they spelled out the possible actions of the men within their families. A woman who made a gift to her son after the death of her husband and then married another man, could revoke the gift for the son's ingratitude. The possible grounds given were if the son tried to cause her death, if he did violence to her, or if he caused her to lose her property. But again, if she lost her good reputation, she lost her legal rights.[26]

Women could, under special circumstances, claim assets of the property of others. When a mother or grandmother had the property of children or grandchildren under her guardianship, and the children had sufficient property for their own support, the mother or grandmother could deduct her expenses from their property. If the children had no property, the mother or grandmother had to care for them out of the goodness of her heart and could not collect expenses. If the woman did not control the property of the children, the children had to state publicly that they wished her expenses to be paid. This law made no provision for the marital status of the woman in question. It was possible, although not common, for the husband to be declared a spendthrift or otherwise incapable of handling the family money, in which case the wife was the most likely candidate to take over the family finances.[27]

There is very little information on women's capability to commit or be held liable for noncriminal wrong-doings (torts). Apparently the man who had authority over the woman, whether father, husband, or other, in most cases took full responsibility for her actions. The Castilians were very concerned about honor and dishonor, and the *Partidas* held that anyone, male or female, over the age of ten and a half years was capable of causing dishonor. Deliberately causing dishonor was an actionable offense, which meant that a suit could be brought in court for damages. The law states that a husband had the right to sue someone for dishonoring his wife, as could a father-in-law for the dishonoring of his daughter-in-law. This makes it appear that these dishonored women could not sue on their own, though some did in New Spain. A man's defense to a suit of this sort was that the good woman had dressed as a bad woman and gone to places frequented by such women. In this case she was at fault and could not sue for being dishonored, so she must have had the right to sue in her own name under ordinary circumstances. Under this construction, those men under whose control she lived could sue also, or if she declined to sue they could bring their own suit, for the dishonor would spread to the whole family.[28]

A husband could not sue his wife for larceny, but he could sue anyone who assisted her in her larcenous actions against him and get compensation from them. He was also allowed to punish his wife so that she would not be tempted to steal from him again. This particular law made no mention of whether the wife could sue the husband for stealing from her, but in other places the wife had the power to enjoin the husband from destroying or wasting her property. A wife could not accuse her husband of adultery, because in Castilian society no injury or dishonor accrued to her. In more modern words: "no harm, no foul." Since she could not prove damages, she could not bring suit against her husband, but she could sue the woman involved.[29]

Castilian women, for the most part, had almost equal legal status with men. By contrast, this was not the case in other parts of Europe, especially in England and those nations, such as the United States, that adopted English common law. As will be demonstrated in later chapters, English common law severely restricted the rights of married women. By law a wife's legal identity was submerged into her husband's: she had no legal existence apart from him.[30]

Under the ideals of the laws of the *Partidas*, women had almost full legal capacity. Women could make contracts and be held to them. They could own both real and personal property. Buying and selling of property by women was common, as evidenced by the presence of forms for these transactions. Castilian women could sue and be sued for civil injuries, though apparently married women usually let their husbands handle these matters. Women were valuable members of the community. Their testimony was trusted and fully admissible in court. By law, and in marked contrast to the rest of Western Europe, there was very little these women could not do.

✶ 3 ✶

Family Law in the Partidas

THIS CHAPTER EXAMINES the laws specifically written to control behavior within the family. This aspect of law is often called domestic relations. Later chapters will show how these domestic relations laws became ingrained in Castilian culture and were transferred to the New World, ending up as part of the Texas legal system.

Part four of the *Partidas* deals in its entirety with domestic relations. There were many detailed laws on the subject of marriage: what constituted a valid marriage; what could annul a marriage; what causes justified a separation or divorce; and what rights married people had in relation to each other and also to those outside the marriage. There were even laws concerning which women could be kept as honorable concubines without benefit of marriage, as well as the rights of concubines.

Castilian society expected women to marry. The only way for a woman to gain honor and dignity was through her husband. A daughter who married a count, thereby becoming a countess, gained much prestige for her family, so most families urged good marriages on their daughters. A father could disinherit a daughter who refused to be married and went to live instead in a brothel, unless he himself delayed the daughter's marriage until she was twenty-five. If that happened, then it was his fault that she was unwed and he could not disinherit her.[1]

Unlike the law in England, under Castilian law parents could not betroth a daughter when she was not present or without her consent. The informed consent of both bride and groom was absolutely necessary to have a valid marriage. A marriage contracted through force or by intimidation of the bride could be annulled by the wronged party, though a woman could validate it if she so desired. It was always necessary to have the consent of the woman's family. A man who married a woman without the consent of her family was placed, along with all of his property, in the power of her nearest relatives, whose only constraint was that they may not kill or severely injure him.[2]

Marriage had to be contracted in good faith by both parties. In most cases, each party to a contract must provide some form of consideration (payment) for the contract to be valid. A dowry was the contractual consideration on the part of the woman that made the marriage contract legally binding. If a woman knew that she could not legally marry a certain man, but nonetheless gave him a dowry, he was not bound by the marriage even though he had accepted the dowry. Because she had not acted in good faith, he did not even have to return the dowry. If both parties knew they could not marry, even though they gave each other gifts for the marriage, the marriage did not exist and the property was forfeited to the Crown. Addressing the ultimate act of bad faith, men who killed their wives for no reason were not allowed to remarry.[3]

A marriage had to be between two people who were physically suited to each other so that the marriage would produce children. If a woman married a man but she was so formed that she could not have conjugal relations with him, then the marriage would be annulled and each would be free to remarry. However, if she remarried and was able to have carnal relations with the second husband, then she was to be removed from the second husband and returned to the first, because the physical impediment had obviously been removed. But if both men were examined and the first husband was so endowed that the woman would still not be able to have relations with him though she could with the second husband, she could remain with the second husband. Another cause for annulment was the impotence or "cold disposition" of the husband that made it unlikely that children would be born to him. In either case, the wife could file for annulment so that she might marry a man who would give her children.[4]

A husband could obtain a divorce from his wife if she was proven to be an adulteress, but the wife could not sue on account of the husband's adultery. Adultery as a crime was defined as when a man had relations with a woman who was married or betrothed to another. The man's marital status was immaterial. The husband was dishonored through his wife's adultery, because it might lead to a child of another man being declared heir to the husband. As mentioned, the woman was not perceived as suffering any dishonor through her husband's relations with another woman, so she was not entitled to sue. A husband could pardon his wife's adultery by continuing to live with her after she promised to reform her behavior, but if she continued her evil ways, he and her other male relatives were obligated to report her to the local government. Otherwise, they would be condoning a mortal sin. There was one protection for a fallen woman: if her husband separated from her for her adultery and then committed the deed himself, she could compel him to return to the marriage.[5]

Most marriages ended with the death of one of the spouses. As mentioned previously, the husband's estate did not include the wife's dowry, her paraphernal property (non-dower property brought into the marriage), or any of her separate property. These would be returned to the wife before any partition of the husband's estate. There were many regulations about wills, stating who could be an heir, who could receive bequests, the proper forms of wills, and so on. If a valid will existed, it controlled the distribution of the estate. If the husband died intestate, that is, without a will, laws governed the distribution of his property. These laws varied according to the status of the people involved. In the unusual event that a rich man married a poor woman, she could claim up to one-quarter of his estate for her maintenance. If she had her own property, however, she could not make this claim. Apparently, in Castile, as elsewhere, marriages usually took place between people of roughly equal social and economic status.[6]

Unless specific action was taken before the death of the spouse, each child would share in the estate, with the eldest son being the main heir. Daughters inherited as well as sons, but if the daughters had already married, their dowry may be subtracted from their share of the estate. If the wife was, or claimed to be, pregnant when the husband died, no distribution could take place until the child was born or it was proved she was not pregnant.[7]

To ensure that the child was truly the issue of the deceased, stringent precautions were taken when a woman claimed to be pregnant at the time of her husband's death. First, trusted women of good reputation examined the widow to see if she was pregnant at the time of his death. If she was, she was closely guarded until she gave birth in front of reputable witnesses, none of whom was allowed to be pregnant. All doors would be locked and guarded during the birth, and no visitors carrying packages would be allowed to enter. If the woman refused to accept these precautions, her child would not inherit unless she could prove conclusively that it belonged to her late husband.[8]

The parentage of children was extremely important to the Castilians. Just as there were laws to ensure that posthumous babies really were the children of the deceased husband, there were laws to prevent the unintentional disinheriting of offspring:

> Women sometimes become so greatly enraged that, through the anger which they entertain against their husbands, they declare that their unborn children, or those who are already born, do not belong to their husbands, but to others.... The said child should not be disinherited, or its rights prejudiced in any way, by speeches of this kind.[9]

On the other hand, women who fraudulently declared the children of others to be their own were guilty of deceit, and the husband and the other heirs could take her to court so that the substituted child would not inherit. Women on the whole, though, were expected to be rational, responsible people, especially when it came to the care of their children. Mothers were in sole control of children less than three years of age, after which they were given to the care of their fathers.[10]

As mentioned, widows were expected to honor the memory of their deceased husbands for at least one year. Those who remarried within this time lost their good reputation, as well as anything they inherited from their first spouse. But there is no indication of any specific length of time that men were supposed to remain unmarried following the death of their wives. Apparently, widowers remarried quickly, especially if there were small children in the household, so that babies could be nurtured by a woman.[11]

Men who could not find a suitable wife did not have to live alone. Concubinage was an integral part of Castilian society, and the concubines, while not as respected as wives, had rights, too. A man could take any free woman as a concubine except one who was virginal, a girl less than twelve years of age, or a widow of good reputation. If he wanted a widow of good reputation to be his concubine, he must state publicly that this was his intention or people would assume that the woman was his wife. A man could only have one concubine at a time, and she must be of such character that he could marry her if he wanted to, that is, she must not be closely related to him or married to another. Although concubines did not personally have the security of status as wife, their children could inherit both from them and from their natural father. Also, there was always the possibility that the man might decide to marry the concubine after all. In this case, their children would become fully legitimate and the former mistress would have all the rights and prerogatives of any other wife.[12]

Family was so important to the Castilians that there were several laws concerning the various levels of legitimacy and inheritability of heirs. At the lowest level of illegitimacy were those children "begotten contrary to law, and in opposition to natural order." These children were those resulting from incestuous unions, those born to women in religious orders, the fruit of adultery, or those whose fathers could not be ascertained. These children's whole existence was deemed so contrary to natural law that they could not be acknowledged by the father and so made legitimate. Not being legitimate meant that a child could not inherit from his or her father, or from anyone in his or her father's line, and such a person could not hold public office.[13]

It was possible for children born during a marriage to be illegitimate, although this was rare. Children born into clandestine marriages were illegitimate if the spouses knew of an impediment that kept them from marrying openly. This impediment made the marriage invalid, and therefore the children were bastards. All marriages that did not meet the dictates of the Catholic Church and were therefore invalid also resulted in offspring being declared illegitimate. Another instance of a child being declared illegitimate was when that child was proved to be the offspring of a man other than his mother's husband. This designation usually resulted from a lawsuit by the husband's true heirs. One more example concerns the offspring of married men. Married men could not legally keep concubines, and so any child born to the concubine of a married man was not, and could not ever be, legitimate.[14]

Single men could keep concubines, and their children were called natural children. Such children could be made legitimate in different ways. The father could take the son to court and declare to the king or council that the child was his and that the son was now devoted to the service of the king or council. This circumstance made the son fully legitimate. He could then inherit and hold office, just as though he were born to a legitimate wife. If a man kept a slave as mistress, he could not legitimate their children unless he first freed the mother, and only then if he had no other legitimate heirs.[15]

A man's natural children could be made legitimate by being so designated in a will, or by other notarized documents. In this case, they could only inherit from their parents and not from other relatives unless specifically mentioned in the other person's will. Natural daughters could be made legitimate by being married to a city official, and children born to a concubine who was faithful to her keeper automatically gained legitimacy if their father married their mother.[16]

All Castilian laws concerning legitimacy are in direct contrast to the common law of England, which held that all children born during a marriage were legitimate and all children born out of a marriage were illegitimate. In England there existed no process for legitimation, though a suspected bastard could be disinherited. There also existed in England no form of adoption, which was popular in war-torn Castile.

As in all other areas, the Spanish laws regarding adoption were specific and detailed. Any free man not under the control of his father could adopt a son. The adopter had to be at least eighteen years older than the adoptee, and the adopter must be able to have his own children. Specifically, he must be physically formed so that he could naturally procreate, and he must not be of a cold disposition, which would prevent his having relations with a woman. However, a man could lose his natural ability to sire children through accident or injury and still be able to adopt.[17]

The adoptee had to consent to the adoption, and so children less than seven years of age could not be adopted, because they did not have the legal capacity to consent. Children between seven and fourteen years old could be adopted with the consent of the king, and the law lists all the things the king should take into consideration before giving consent. Freedmen could not be adopted because of the loyalty they owed to the master who freed them and because the former slave could be re-enslaved if the master wished. Guardians could not adopt their minor wards because guardians had to render accounts of their wards' property and adoptive fathers did not for fear that the adoptive father planned to steal from his adopted son. After the ward reached the age of twenty-five years, however, the guardian could adopt him if the king consented. In this case the ward would not be defrauded by the guardian.[18]

There were no laws regarding the adoption of daughters, so apparently this did not happen. The purpose of adoption was to give a man an heir, and while women could inherit, males were customarily the main heirs of the father. The only thing that would be accomplished by the adoption of a daughter would be to split the inheritance and oblige the father to provide another dowry. Neither of these outcomes made monetary sense. As noted earlier, women could not adopt except to replace a son who had been lost in battle. This restriction suggests that having a male heir was more important to the Castilians, for while women were valuable members of the family, the sons carried the family honor. When a daughter married into another family, she became part of that family, while a son remained his father's son.[19]

Family law also dealt with circumstances that were not as felicitous as adoption. Adultery, for example, was both a crime and a family affair and was handled in both sections of the law. What survived into twentieth-century Texas as "the unwritten law" of husbands was set down in the *Partidas*. If a husband found his wife in the act of committing adultery, the husband had the right to kill the other man. He did not have the right, however, to kill his wife. Instead he must turn her over to a judge. If a husband suspected that a man was trying to wrong him through his wife, the husband must notify the suspected adulterer three times, ordering him not to speak to his wife, and the husband had to tell the wife not to speak to the other man. After these warnings, if the wife and the other man were found together, adultery was presumed to have taken place. In this instance, the husband would be justified in killing the other man, but he still was not allowed to kill his wife.[20]

When a husband suspected his wife of adultery, it was his moral duty to accuse her so that she would stop committing a mortal sin. After the adultery was proved, he could either divorce her or pardon her. All that was needed to pardon her was his continuing to live with her. If she continued to commit adultery after the husband pardoned her, her father, brothers, and uncles could accuse her of the offense, because her actions brought dishonor upon them.[21]

A man who committed adultery with a married woman was subject to severest punishment. Even if the husband did not kill the adulterer, the law could take his life. The automatic penalty for a man convicted of adultery was death. For a woman, the automatic penalty was public scourging, after which she would be sent to a convent, and she had to forfeit her dowry.[22]

Several defenses could be mounted to challenge the charge of adultery. If the man did not know that the woman was married, he could not be convicted of adultery. The woman, on the other hand, would still be guilty because she knew she was married. If, however, she believed that her husband was dead, she could not be convicted of adultery. In another scenario, if the husband was the procurer for the act of adultery, or if he consented to it, he could not accuse his wife. But this was a chancy defense, because any man who acted as procurer for his wife would be put to death, as would any person who acted as a procurer for any good woman. A woman's poor reputation would apparently act as a defense for the Christian man who committed adultery with her. When a Jewish man had carnal relations with a Christian woman, no matter what her reputation, he would be put to death. When a Moor had relations with a Christian woman, no matter what her reputation, he would be stoned to death. In both cases the woman would forfeit half of her property and be publicly scourged for the first offense. The penalty for the second offense was death.[23]

Society also discouraged acts of seduction not culminating in adultery. It was a crime for a man to importune virgins, married women, or honorable widows. This would lead them to be suspected of dishonor, and the man was liable to punishment. When a man gave a gift "to a woman of good reputation for the purpose of inducing her to commit acts of wickedness with her body," she did not have to return the gift, even if she did not commit the act of wickedness. The man's base conduct nullified the implied contract. Likewise, if a man gave a gift to a woman of poor reputation for the same reason, he could not recover the gift from her either, because her sin lay not in accepting gifts but in lying with men. Since she did not commit a base act but he did, he forfeited the gift to her.[24]

Men and women had complete equality in one respect: the penalty for a wife killing her husband was the same as for the husband killing the wife—death. A woman who induced her own abortion by drugs or physical means was guilty of murder only if the child was already moving in the womb. Also, any man, including her husband, who struck her after the fetus had begun to move and by his violence caused an abortion was guilty of murder. Even after a woman was accused of heinous crimes, she still had some legal protection. Accused women were not put into prison with men but were kept in convents, so that in the case that they were judged innocent they would not have been dishonored.[25]

Some murders were justified by the circumstances. A father could kill a man who was in the act of having sex with his daughter, and a husband could kill a man caught in the act of having sex with his wife. In both cases, the father or husband would consider the woman "violated" whether the act was consensual or not. A cuckolded husband could kill the man who was committing adultery with the husband's wife, but the father of a misguided daughter was more restricted. If a father found his daughter committing adultery, he had two options. Legally, he could kill both parties or kill neither. It was considered unfair to a wronged husband, who had suffered the greater dishonor but who could not kill his wife, for a father to fail to kill his daughter if he killed the daughter's lover. As any good defense attorney would note, however, the difference between violation and adultery lies only in the mind of the woman, and it would be much in her self-interest to claim rape.[26]

Law-abiding Castilians considered it a horrible crime for a man to carry off a virgin, married woman, widow, or woman belonging to a religious order. Any such action brought dishonor to all the woman's relatives and represented violence against both honorable people and honorable society. The penalty for carrying off and dishonoring such a woman was death, and all the man's property was forfeited to the woman. If the woman consented to marry her abductor, he would not be killed, but if her parents did not consent to the marriage, his property would go to them. Consent of both parties and the family of the woman was usually necessary to have a valid marriage, but in this case the marriage was valid after the nonconsenting parents received the man's property.[27]

From the *Partidas,* the reader can discern several things about medieval Castilian society. First, they believed the rule of law was necessary for an orderly, stable community. Since Castilians had a great propensity for bringing lawsuits to avenge every slight, a system of laws that insured justice for all was the bedrock of the society.

The family was the basic unit of the community, and the laws tended to augment the stability of that unit. All members of the family knew their places, their duties, and their privileges. Children were important. Their rights were protected by law. They could own property, but their parent or guardian would administer it, since minors were presumed incapable by law and might be taken advantage of by unscrupulous people. The guardians themselves were subject to charges of malfeasance and liable for any wastage of the child's property. Women were valuable members of the community and had the right to consent to, if not choose, their husbands, for again no marriage was valid without their consent.

Many of the laws affecting women reflect the concern of the society that the children born to a married woman were also the children of her husband. This concern brought about stringent adultery laws, where no actual proof was needed if the circumstances were suspicious enough. Women could lose their reputations, could even become criminals, and still not face the same harsh penalties as their male counterparts. A woman had to be irredeemable to face the death penalty, while men could receive capital punishment merely for inflicting dishonor. Women, even as criminals, had value. Honorable women were the most priceless possessions of the family, the community, and the realm.

In retrospect, Castilian women had specific legal rights under the *Partidas* that were much greater than those of women in many other countries and times. These women did not have total freedom, for they had to abide by all the rules of their community in order to claim their legal rights. As long as they kept within the framework of society, however, they could call on the law for protection from anyone who would take away those rights. Castilian women knew their rights and their limitations and how they could make even the limitations work for them. They would take this knowledge with them to the New World.

★ 4 ★

The Transfer of Castilian Laws to New Spain

BY THE FIFTEENTH CENTURY, when Ferdinand and Isabella joined the Crowns of Aragon and Castile, the laws of the *Partidas* were accepted as the customary law by the people of Castile. Though the *Partidas* were not the only laws, as each town was still governed by its own codes, they did serve as a common law for all of Castile. It was the goal of the Catholic monarchs to have "One Faith, One Crown, One Law" for all of Spain. They only partially realized this goal during their lifetimes. Ferdinand and Isabella never had the control over their Spanish subjects that they exercised over their people in the overseas possessions. This chapter deals with the "One Law" they wished to apply to all their subjects, including those in the New World, and its basis in the *Partidas*.

The year 1492 was a watershed year in Spanish history. The Sephardic Jews had to leave Spain or convert to Christianity. The final phase of the Reconquest was completed, and the Moors no longer ruled the kingdom of Granada. The "One Faith" had been accomplished. The entire Iberian Peninsula, except for Portugal and Navarre, was nominally united under Ferdinand and Isabella. So they had established the "One Crown," though their actual authority was limited within Spain itself. The work *Arte de la lengua castellana* standardized and modernized the Castilian vernacular. And lastly, an excellent navigator and self-promoter named Christopher Columbus persuaded Isabella to finance his journey to the East Indies by sailing west.

Because Isabella, the queen of Castile, underwrote this exploration, when new lands were found the "One Law" that governed those possessions was Castilian in origin. It was Castilians who populated the islands and mainlands of the New World, and it was the Castilian way of life that spread over the western hemisphere from the southern part of present-day United States to the tip of South America, excluding Brazil. Technically, Castilians were the only legal emigrants to the Indies until 1600.

The Castilians developed a science of law early because their way of life depended on rational, reasonable laws. The *cortes* (parliament) of 1480 ordered the famous jurist Alfonso Díaz de Montalvo to codify the existing Castilian laws. The result was the *Ordenanzes Reales* (Royal Ordinances) that became the basis of modern Spanish jurisprudence. The Laws of Toro in 1505 stated that everyone who would be using the laws, such as lawyers and judges, had to be familiar with the *Partidas,* the *Fuero Real* (Royal Codes), and the *Ordenamientos* (laws and edicts) passed by Ferdinand and Isabella. Thus, instead of relying on medieval jurists or the caprice of judges as in other European countries, everyone would follow the same laws. Even the Crown knew and followed the laws. Ferdinand and Isabella owned two copies of the *Partidas,* a printed copy and a manuscript made especially for them. They also owned copies of the *Fuero Real,* the *Ordenamientos,* books on canon law, books on civil law, and commentaries on many different kinds of law.[1]

The laws passed by Ferdinand and Isabella were "designed to buttress royal authority and maintain social stability." Laws rested not only on the strength of the monarchs but also on the weight of authorities cited. For example, the *Partidas* cited the authority of the Old and New Testaments, the Church Fathers, and the commentaries of Roman jurists, as well as traditional Castilian customs. Ferdinand and Isabella followed this tradition by consulting authorities before making decisions. This practice added weight to their edicts and increased the prestige of the monarchy. The Catholic monarchs realized that the law, when it was in line with religion, political reality, and national purpose, was a mighty weapon. During their reign, written law supported the monarchy and the monarchy supported written law. Justice was therefore a royal instrument.[2]

The *Partidas* were particularly useful in this regard because they placed the king as absolute ruler over each of his vassals. There was a direct link between the king and each vassal, not a pyramid downward from king to chief vassal, to lesser vassal, to least vassal. Through the *Partidas,* Ferdinand and Isabella espoused total royal sovereignty. In Spain itself they had to compromise with powerful lords and other interests, but in the New World monarchy was unchallenged. Little separated the Crown from the Church. The Crown upheld the Church and the law, and the people held the two in almost equal regard. The law itself was almost religious in character: people believed in the law as the way to maintain an ordered and peaceful society. The law was so important to Queen Isabella that she incorporated a directive into her will in 1504 to recodify the laws of

Castile. That this was not accomplished until the reign of Philip II in 1567 points out the pace of Spanish bureaucracy rather than lack of support for the project.[3]

Within Spain, even within Castile, Isabella had to contend with powerful nobles and church officials. She was determined, however, that nothing come between her and her right to rule. In the New World this was much more easily accomplished. Technically, the New World belonged to the Crown of Castile. The viceroyalties of New Spain (Colonial Mexico) and Peru joined with other Castilian possessions to form an empire governed by the laws of that realm. The Crown was absolute possessor of all political and property rights from the beginning, and it soon gained religious power as well.[4]

Ferdinand and Isabella were both intensely religious and jealous of their powers. Though they were called the Catholic

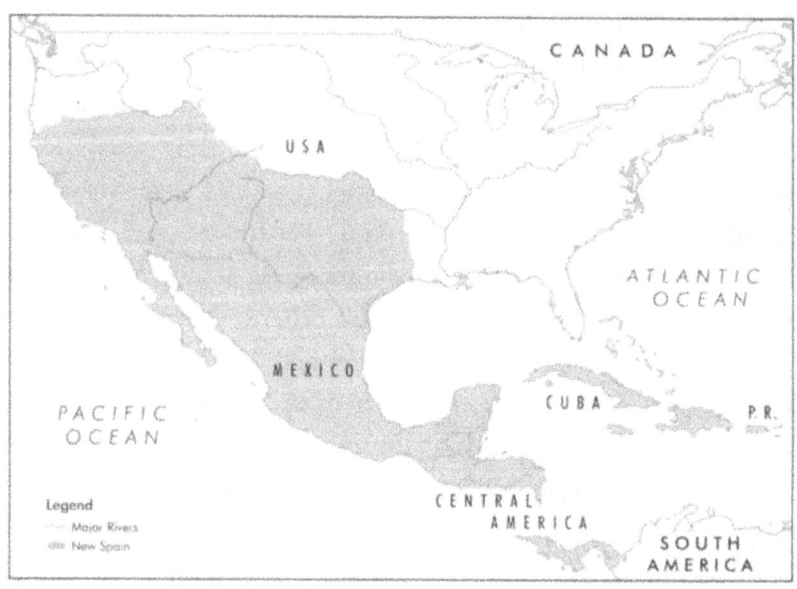

New Spain.

Kings, they did not want the Church to encroach on their royal prerogatives. From the beginning of Spanish exploration in the New World, the Crown of Castile sought total control. The monarchy achieved this in the *Patronato Real* (Royal Patronage). In 1493 Pope Alexander VI began the process of transferring control of church matters in the New World to the Crown. In 1493 the pope also divided the New World and Asia between Spain and Portugal; the line of demarcation was moved in 1494 when Castile and Portugal signed the Treaty of Tordesillas. The unexpected result of that treaty was to award Brazil to Portugal. The papal bulls of 1501 and 1508 spelled out the rights of the kings in their new territory. In all of the newly discovered lands, the Crown controlled taxation of church property and the nomination of all higher church officials. The pope could only select from the Crown's short list of nominees for bishops, archbishops, and abbots. Crown-appointed viceroys and governors nominated lower church officials to New World prelates.[5]

In return for these privileges, the Crown pledged to spread the Roman Catholic faith throughout all its new possessions. The Crown paid the cost of building and operating churches, monasteries, and charitable hospitals. It received all revenues from church activities, but these were never enough to cover their expenses. Papal bulls and other religious instructions had to be approved by the Council of the Indies before they could be announced in the New World. In effect, the Church became another branch of Castilian government in the expanding empire. As conquistadors opened new areas to Spain, the Crown set up new bishoprics and dioceses. The viceroys who ruled New Spain also ruled the Church within New Spain, leaving Rome very little influence there.[6]

In the decades of exploration, the most important reason for clergy to come to the New World was to convert the natives to Catholicism. Franciscans (beginning in 1523), Dominicans (1526), Augustinians (1533), and later Jesuits (1572–1767) in New Spain fervently sought conversions and accepted the risk of martyrdom. The Crown paid for the passage and provisions of friars to the New World and provided food and shelter until they could form a stable community. Because so few secular clergy came to the Americas in the first decades, papal bulls allowed lesser clergy to perform sacraments normally reserved for regular clergy. A clergyman could baptize thousands of Indians, sometimes hundreds of thousands, during his sojourn in America. An estimated four million Indians received the sacrament of baptism during the first fifteen years of Spanish conquest. Most, perhaps almost all, of these Indians received very little religious instruction before their baptism. When the Indians reverted to their previous way of life after being claimed by the Catholic Church, the clergy viewed them as heretics. Heresy, especially such widespread apostasy, brought in the Inquisition.[7]

Few institutions have gained such a poor reputation as the Spanish Inquisition. Pope Sixtus IV authorized the creation of an inquisition under state control in 1478 when Isabella petitioned for a way to control the "menace" of converted Jews in Castile. Jews had, for centuries, been protected throughout the Iberian Peninsula. However, a combination of anti-Semitism sweeping Europe in the fourteenth and fifteenth centuries, the economic and political power of the Jewish community that might oppose the Crown, and the intense desire of Ferdinand and Isabella to have a state unified in religion as well as politics made a state-controlled Inquisition viable. The populace felt threatened both by Jews and by *conversos,* persons of Jewish heritage who had converted to Catholicism. The *conversos* were especially suspect because they claimed to be Christian while often secretly practicing their traditional religion, or so many people believed. The primary purpose of the Spanish Inquisition was to weed out heretics. It therefore did not apply to non-Christians, whether Jewish, Muslim, or pagan. According to both church and state, people who had been converted to Christianity but who then practiced another religion were heretical apostates. *Conversos* were the first target of the Inquisition, but this reasoning applied as well to Indians in the New World.[8]

One interesting insight into the Spanish psychology of this era was that even the lowest classes felt themselves part of the dominant warrior class. They did not feel humble and downtrodden. People in the lower classes strongly identified themselves as Catholic Christians, and therefore honorable. The poor people obviously had pure blood because the popular view held that all converted Jews were rich. This belief gave even the poorest peasants reason to be proud, since their very poverty affirmed the purity of their lineage. A tradition of having a military heritage, even when none actually existed in a particular family, and the custom of thinking of themselves as living on the front line of the battle to extend Christianity, proved useful to the settlers of the New World.[9]

As soon as the Catholic Church came to the New World, it began converting the Indians. Clergymen whose mission it was to baptize all inhabitants of the New World and so save their souls were ardent, eager, and sincere. They could not understand why, after natives had been baptized, they would return to their previous faith. In 1517 the Inquisitor General of Spain, Cardinal Jiménez de Cisneros, granted inquisitorial powers to bishops in the Indies so that they would have the authority to deal with these heretics. Bishop Manso of Puerto Rico and Pedro de Córdova, a Dominican, became official inquisitors for the Indies in 1519. The Dominicans exercised most of the inquisitorial functions until the formal Spanish Inquisition arrived in New Spain in 1571. This was also the year that Indians were removed from the power of the Inquisition, due to the New Laws of Philip II. Again, the primary function of the Inquisition was to safeguard the purity of the faith and protect good Spanish citizens from the contamination of heretical thinking, especially after the successes of the Protestant Reformation.[10]

Most Spanish citizens of New Spain actually welcomed the coming of the Inquisition. During the time of the Reformation and Counter-Reformation, Spanish Catholics hated and feared Protestants as well as other heretics. The lower classes of the New World, much like the lower classes throughout Europe, feared the upper classes, especially those suspected of being secret Jews. When the Inquisition came to each community, those secret Jews would be exposed and punished, or so the populace believed. Known heretics would leave villages and towns before the arrival of the Inquisition, much to the relief of the orthodox. Because the Inquisition punished such sins as public drunkenness, cursing, lewd behavior, and other social improprieties, upright citizens saw the Inquisition as a way to rid themselves of undesirables. The Spanish culture of that time valued conformity, and the Inquisition helped to promote compliance.[11]

Queen Isabella zealously guarded her rights and privileges in the Indies as well as in Castile. All movement between Spain and the Spanish empire in the New World was tightly controlled by the *Casa de Contratación* (House of Trade), established by the Crown in 1503 and housed in Seville until the early

1700s. Seville was, for many years, the only authorized port for passage or shipping to and from the New World. One of the main functions of the *Casa de Contratación* was to check out the background of potential emigrants. Each person had to prove his or her *limpieza de sangre,* or purity of blood. Only persons who could prove that their heritage was fully Christian (i.e., no *conversos*), received a license to travel to the New World. As mentioned, at first only Castilians were allowed to travel to the New World, but this restriction was relaxed around 1600 to include all properly licensed Spaniards. Still, only persons born in Spain itself were supposed to emigrate to New Spain. Other subjects of the Spanish empire had to obtain special dispensation from the king to cross the Atlantic legally.[12]

Another function of the *Casa de Contratación* was the censorship of books shipped to the New World. The purpose of this censorship was again to ensure the purity and uniformity of thought in the Indies. Officials forbade shipment of heretical works, including any by Protestant authors. Later, works praising the American or French revolutions also had to be smuggled into the Indies, as did certain philosophical and intellectual works that the House of Trade officials deemed controversial.[13]

In 1524 Charles V created the *Consejo Real de las Indies* (Royal Council of the Indies) to govern and administer the New World. This agency traveled with the Spanish court and turned the wishes of the Crown into law for all Castilian overseas possessions. Shortly after Columbus's return from his first voyage, Isabella put her own chaplain, Juan Rodríguez de Fonseca, in charge of all matters relating to the New World. Fonseca remained in this capacity, personally managing these activities and reporting directly to the Crown, until his death in 1524, though the *Casa de Contratación* took over immediate supervision of all matters related to trade. When Charles V came to the throne, and especially when he became emperor, he had little time to give to the Indies. As he did in other situations, Charles V created a royal council to take over bureaucratic functions.[14]

In the beginning, the council was rather small, with a president, four councilors who were either lawyers or clergy, and a few clerks, including a secretary, an accountant, a reporter, and an usher. Later, as more issues needed to be decided, the council grew to include a grand chancellor and his deputy, more accountants, more lawyers, more reporters, more ushers, a chaplain, notaries, and even a historian. Eventually there were ten councilors and an even more numerous staff. In actuality, the Council of the Indies became the most important royal council, though it remained in secondary position in honor to the Council of Castile. The Council of the Indies had the same supreme authority over the New World as the Council of Castile did over Spain itself. The Indies belonged directly to the Crown of Castile, and only the council could issue laws regarding these lands. By the authority of the *Patronato Real,* the council even approved papal bulls before they could be read in the New World.[15]

The Council of the Indies held final legal authority over the colonies as well. It sat as the court of last resort on any matter pertaining to the Indies, including civil and criminal cases arising in the New World. All Indians were in the charge of the council, and it decided cases regarding abuses in the *encomiendas,* where the early *encomenderos* received the right to native labor. *Encomienda* was a grant of labor and tribute made by the Crown to conquistadors and other favored people. The native people were forced to do a certain amount of labor each year and provide a certain amount of tribute, which varied from place to place and time to time. The *encomendero* was supposed to provide religious instruction and defend the native people from outside attackers. The system was widely abused and later outlawed, but it persisted anyway. The council also arranged for *residencias,* a review of each high official's conduct at the end of his term in office, *visitadores,* or inspectors who reported on any and every aspect of life in the Spanish colonies, and the exercise of royal patronage within the Indies. Because the council's workload was so enormous and because officials had to act carefully to avoid personal responsibility for misdeeds, the council acted slowly. The council's orders, rulings, and laws were compiled and published over the several centuries of Spanish dominion in the Americas.[16]

Over time, these orders, rulings, and laws grew so voluminous and contradictory that even lawyers could not determine the applicability of statutes in any particular case. The king and council decided that a systematic compilation was necessary. Juan de Ovando had just completed an inspection of the Indies and reported that members of the council had inadequate knowledge of the Indies. Philip II ordered him to undertake this project. Ovando organized the task and completed one book on the ordinances of the Council of the Indies before he was promoted to the presidency of the council and stopped work on the compilation. It took several men, most notably Antonio de León Pinelo, more than a hundred years to accomplish this work, and in 1681, the first four-volume collection of colonial edicts was published. It contained only 6,400 laws, reduced from almost half a million royal decrees. Later editions revised the *Recopilación* to include new laws and omit legislation no longer in force. This study uses the *Recopilación de las Leyes,* or

Compilation of Laws, published in 1791, because it contains the compilation of laws most applicable for the period 1717–1773, the early years of San Fernando de Béxar, which will be discussed in later chapters.[17]

The *Recopilación* deals primarily with administration and bureaucracy. Much like the *Partidas,* the first book of the *Recopilación* covers the Church, its rights and responsibilities, and its limits in the new lands. Book Two pertains to the administration of the Indies, the various officials, and their duties. Book Three incorporates the military establishment and its jurisdictional limits. The legalities of the process of discovery, exploration, and exploitation of the Indies is contained in Book Four, while Book Five presents more detail about the duties of the minor officials, as well as the other professional people of the cities. Book Six considers the rights of the Indians and of the *encomenderos,* those Spaniards who had the right to collect Indian tribute. Various unsavory persons, such as vagabonds and Gypsies, are the topic of Book Seven, and Book Eight explains royal rights and privileges in the New World. The last book, Book Nine, covers a wide variety of topics, including expected behavior of the officials of the *Real Audiencias* (Royal Courts), the *Casa de Contratación* (House of Trade) that governed who came from and went to the Indies, the various offices that had to be created for the frontier situation, and even the navy. In all of these books, the laws are handled with the same detail and precision found in the *Partidas,* with the Council of the Indies trying to foresee all possible events and promulgate laws to cover them.

The Spanish Crown did not try to change Castilian society as it spread out in its overseas possessions. Instead, it was determined to enlarge the scope of that society and purify it at the same time. The *Casa de Contratación* required proof of purity of lineage before it would grant licenses to go abroad. People who were considered undesirable in Spain were not allowed to emigrate to the Indies. Such undesirable people included recent converts, Jews, Moors, Gypsies and other wanderers, foreigners, and heretics. Single women, too, were not allowed to make the journey overseas, but the rules encouraged, and sometimes mandated, that married men bring their wives to the Indies, or send for them as soon as the husbands became established settlers.[18]

One way in which Castilian society differed from the rest of Europe was the traditional legal status of women; this feature, like so many other cultural elements imported from Castile, proved useful in the New World. As in the *Partidas,* only in exceptional cases did women have full civil capacity. As single women they were under the control of their fathers, older brothers, or uncles. As married women, they were under the control of their husbands. But as widows, responsible, respectable women could gain full capacity. Regarding women's rights, as Castilians carried their laws to the Indies, no special difference was made between the laws of the peninsula and the laws of the Indies. The Council of the Indies did draft a few regulations pertaining to the status of the wives, daughters, and wards of Spanish officials, as well as those pertaining to women's rights to go to the New World. The council also issued regulations to protect Indian women. But as a whole, lawmakers for the Indies intended to carry over the traditional community property rights of women, because these had served so well during the Reconquest. The right of community property had helped repopulate the lands gained from the Moors and therefore should work just as well in populating the New World with

Castilians. In fact, these rights spread with the Spanish into what would become the American Southwest.[19]

The laws of the *Consejo Real* extended many of the traditional protections and privileges of Castilian women to the women of New Spain. These protections could also be adapted to the new situations. The Spanish administrators of the New World saw the natives as having the right of governmental protection from private abuse. In the *encomienda* system, Indian women did receive some protection. Those women could not be locked up and forced to spin and weave clothing for the *encomenderos*. When Indian men worked on the ranches of the *encomenderos*, the native wives and children could not be forced to work also. If they wished to work, they had to be paid, for their labor was not part of *encomienda* privilege.[20]

Because honor was so important to the Spanish, insofar as it was possible the honor of Indian women was also protected. No married native woman could be forced to work in the house of a male Spaniard, unless her husband was also a servant in the same household. If a woman working as a house servant married, the *encomendero* could not refuse to let her go live with her husband. And no single woman could be a house servant unless both she and her parents freely consented. This restriction reflects the necessity for both a woman and her family to consent to a marriage, as set forth in the *Partidas*.[21]

One of the main goals of the conquerors was to Christianize the Indians, and this obligation included inducing them to live by Castilian standards. The native family structure was to be replaced by the Castilian model, and the laws would punish any deviations or lapses. By law, no Indian of either gender could have more than one spouse, and those who did so were to be punished as an example to others. No chief, even if still an infidel, was allowed to have more than one wife. Furthermore, Indians were not allowed to continue the practice of selling their children into marriages. Instead, the Spanish way, where consent was required, was to be used. Indian women, unlike Castilian women, did not have much legal capacity or responsibility, so they did not have to pay taxes even when they were the heads of household.[22]

Spanish women in the Indies kept their traditional rights of inheritance and property ownership. Widows could inherit *encomiendas* from their husbands, provided there was no legitimate male heir. Legitimate daughters, if of age, could also inherit *encomiendas*, provided they were married or did marry within a year of the death of their husband. These constraints were expressly designed to keep helpless young women from being victimized by unscrupulous men. Similar protections for more experienced widows apparently were not needed. A further limitation was added, stipulating that in order for a spouse of either gender to succeed to the *encomienda*, he or she must have lived there as the spouse for at least six months. This proviso again served to assure that the property not pass into the hands of unscrupulous persons.[23]

The Spanish Crown wanted the new lands to be settled and peaceful, and therefore profitable. It recognized the value of wives and family in controlling the uncivilized impulses of the conquistadors. Consequently, the rules on bringing wives to the New World became stricter as time went on. By a law announced in 1539, single women were not allowed licenses to go abroad, and married women who went overseas had to go directly to their husbands. In 1546 the law allowed men to take their wives with them when they went to the Indies. By 1549 married men could not serve in any official capacity overseas unless they took their wives with them. After 1554 wives could get licenses on their own from the *Casa de Contratación* to join their husbands in the new lands. Even merchants who traded in the New World, except for their first, exploratory voyage, had to take their wives with them.[24]

Though the Council of the Indies made the actual rules for the New World, it did so in accordance with the wishes of the Crown. Therefore, the personalities and temperaments of different rulers contributed to the style of administration of the colonial possessions. Ferdinand and Isabella gave personal attention to the progress of exploration and the founding of colonies in the Indies, although not much activity had taken place by the end of Ferdinand's reign in 1516. Charles V, as emperor of the Holy Roman Empire, had a much larger area to rule and was determined to rule each of his possessions by its own laws. One effect of this decision was to stop all constitutional changes during his rule. Another was the development of a new bureaucracy within each territory to carry out his directives. Charles V created the Council of the Indies because the old-style manner of government was not adequate to the new workload.[25]

As noted, the Council of the Indies had complete control over all judicial, administrative, and ecclesiastical affairs in the Indies. However, the Crown did not want any branch of government to become too powerful, so there was a system of checks on the various governmental powers in the Indies. Government by *audiencias*, or courts, was limited by the authority of the viceroyalties, and vice versa. After the reign of Charles V, these checks evolved into governmental stalemate, as indecisiveness became the hallmark of the Hapsburgs, especially Philip II, who approved almost every detail in his own handwriting.[26]

During the rule of the later Hapsburgs, various local powers in the Spanish realms often tried to become more autonomous. In the colonies, this meant the growth of some local control, but this condition did not last long. When the Bourbons came to the throne in 1700, their goal was to improve the economic and social stability of the country. They instituted moral progress, material prosperity, and colonial reform. They enhanced the power of the Crown, which had diminished under the later Hapsburgs, in order to achieve their purposes. The Bourbons followed the tradition of Ferdinand and Isabella in imposing royal control over the Church, especially in the colonies. The Bourbon kings unified Spain through prosperity and religion. Their enlightened despotism was good for the country and for the Indies, ending decades of bureaucratic lassitude.[27]

Colonial administration, then, was based on the laws of Castile and administered by a bureaucracy that usually acted with glacial slowness. These repeated bureaucratic delays led the people in the Indies to rely more on traditional laws, as stated in the *Partidas,* than on governmental regulations. The area of women's status did not receive much governmental attention and thus remained true to the tradition of the *Partidas.* Women retained all their rights in Spain's overseas possessions and were acknowledged as vital to the civilization of the New World.

★ 5 ★

The Spanish Legal System Arrives in Texas

TEXAS WAS ONE of the last Spanish provinces founded in North America. Though it had been discovered and the coast mapped by Alonso Alvarez de Pineda in 1519 and had been explored involuntarily by Cabeza de Vaca and his castaway friends from 1528 to 1535, it was not until the French presented a threat to the valuable interior provinces that the Spanish decided to settle Texas. The first such threat was René Robert Cavelier, Sieur de La Salle, who founded a colony on Matagorda Bay in 1685. That colony was short-lived, though it generated much excitement among Spanish officials. The later entrance of Frenchman Louis Juchereau de St. Denis into Texas in 1714 provided direct motivation for the Spanish government to establish missions and presidios in East Texas. Father Francisco Hidalgo, who first entered Texas in 1691, had also long wanted to reestablish missions among the Tejas Indians. This combination of a French threat and a desire to save the Indians' souls finally led to the permanent settlement of Texas by Spaniards in 1716.[1]

Meanwhile, the continued presence of the French in Louisiana, dating from 1699, as well as their persistence in seeking trade opportunities within Spanish territories, prompted colonial officials in Mexico City to establish frontier missions as a deterrent to foreign encroachment. As early as January 1, 1700, the first Río Grande mission, San Juan Bautista, was established at present-day Guerrero, Coahuila. Two other missions soon took root in the same area. And by 1703, Presidio San Juan Bautista provided protection for the nearby religious outposts.[2]

Although Texas had been abandoned by Spaniards in 1693, the province and its native population were never far from the minds of Franciscan priests stationed at the Río Grande missions. An exploratory expedition to the north of the Great River in 1709 noted the suitability of an area near the confluence of the San Antonio River and San Pedro Creek as a mission site. Then, in direct response to the French threat from Louisiana, six missions and a presidio were set up in East Texas in 1716–1717.[3]

Still missing, however, was a way station between the Río Grande missions and those located in East Texas and western Louisiana. That omission was corrected in 1718 with the founding of Mission San Antonio de Valero and Presidio San Antonio de Béxar near the headwaters of the San Antonio River. Of greater significance to this study was a third outpost known as Villa de Béxar, where the families of presidio soldiers and a few civilians resided.[4]

During the years 1718 through 1731, the population began to grow. Mission records at Mission San Antonio de Valero indicate that 47 couples were married and 107 children were baptized at that mission alone. The civilian population also grew,

The Spanish Legal System Arrives in Texas

but slowly. The total population in 1726 was about two hundred. By 1731 there were twenty-five civilian households, composed mostly of ex-soldiers who had brought their families to the area and remained there after they retired. These settlers farmed, raised livestock, and protected themselves from Indians. The total population in 1730 was three hundred. The presidial commander was the sole source of authority, for no civilian government had been established. But this situation was about to change.[5]

In 1724 Brigadier General Pedro de Rivera y Villalón had left Mexico City to tour the presidios and missions of the entire region that was the northern frontier of New Spain. Rivera's instructions were to study the defenses of the frontier and find ways to save money. Presidial captains had a reputation for corruption and dishonesty and had often been accused of misusing their authority. For example, soldiers had to buy all their equipment from the commanders and were vastly overcharged for their gear. Captains also used soldiers as laborers on their private lands. Some presidios had outlived their purpose, for the nearby Indians had either been pacified or had died out. In all, Brigadier General Rivera toured twenty-three outposts over the course of three and a half years and filed reports on each one. His reports on the Texas presidios had an immense impact on the future of Spanish settlement in that province.[6]

As part of his official recommendations following his inspection of all Spanish military garrisons, Rivera recommended a significant reduction in the number of soldiers stationed in Texas, including those at Presidio San Antonio de Béxar. Although soldiers stationed at San Antonio were actually fit for duty, as opposed to the majority of soldiers in other presidios, that area was so peaceful that fewer soldiers were needed. He recommended closing a presidio in East Texas and reducing the size of the other garrisons. In all, the total number of soldiers in Texas was reduced by 150 presidials. Three of the six missions in East Texas, which had had little success in Christianizing Indians and which were on the verge of extinction, were closed and moved to San Antonio in 1731.[7]

The overall effect of the Rivera report was to save money for the king, but it also slowed the progress of settlement in Texas. With peace in Europe between France and Spain, the French threat seemed less dire, and the Indians were temporarily tranquil. Accordingly, the Spanish government had concluded that a large military occupation of Texas was inappropriate and expensive. What were really needed were civilian settlers to more effectively populate Texas. But few people in New Spain wanted to move to a frontier where there were so few soldiers to protect them from potentially hostile Indians. Instead, the king and the Council of the Indies decided to bring four hundred families over from Galicia in northwest Spain and the Canary Islands to help settle Spanish Texas.[8]

However, four hundred families who wanted to move to the isolated, relatively unpopulated frontier could not be found. In fact, only fifteen families, numbering fifty-five persons, made the trip from the Canary Islands to found the villa of San Fernando de Béxar. En route they suffered many hardships before arriving on March 9, 1731.

Just as was done when cities in medieval Spain had wanted to attract residents during the Reconquest, promises were made to these Texas immigrants. The Spanish Crown offered the Canary Islanders these inducements: First, they would be named to the rank of hidalgo, meaning a "son of somebody," the lowest rank of the nobility. They would receive free land, seed, and necessary tools with which to raise crops, and the important right to elect their own municipal government. Each family was then to receive ten ewes and a ram, ten goats and a buck, five sows and a boar, and five cows and a bull. All of these promises would lead to legal disputes within a short time. The newly created hidalgos, while they expected to work, also expected to be treated with respect due their new rank, which was not always forthcoming from men in the presidio or mission.[9]

When the settlers arrived, their first task was to plant crops, which would provide food for the coming winter season. Since there was no time to dig new *acequias,* or irrigation ditches, the Islanders settled near the ditches dug by the older inhabitants of San Antonio. On July 2, 1731, the town site was surveyed and laid out. Streets were forty *varas* (thirty-three and one-third inches) wide, house lots were eighty *varas* square. On July 20 all the Islanders were formally recognized as *Hijos Dalgo.*[10]

By order of the viceroy, don Juan Antonio Pérez de Almazán, captain of the presidio of San Antonio de Béxar, named the eldest and most respectable men to the offices of the *cabildo,* or city government. Juan Leal Goraz was the first *regidor,* or councilman. The other council members were Juan Curbelo, Antonio Salvas, Salvador Rodríguez, Manuel de Nis, and Juan Leal Jr. These first officials held their offices for life, or until they resigned. Vicente Alvarez Travieso was the first sheriff, and Francisco de Arocha was named secretary to the council and notary public. The first election in Texas was for the two alcaldes, or magistrates, to be chosen from among the council members. Juan Leal Goraz was the first alcalde, and Salvador Rodríguez was the second.[11]

The laws of the *Recopilación* detailed the method for setting up and maintaining a city government, and the establishment of the villa of San Fernando de Béxar violated several of these laws. This violation should not be interpreted as meaning that the villa was lawless, rather that the Spanish recognized that the laws had to suit the surroundings to be effective. The first rule to be violated was that the villa was established very close to a mission. The law specified that there be at least five leagues (thirteen miles) between settlements, but the fierceness of the Apache Indians made a compact settlement safer. The appointment and election of officials did not proceed according to the law either. Some city officials were supposed to be appointed for life, but they soon were elected annually. Because of the small number of settlers, and because many offices were by that time sold in perpetuity, the law was disregarded. After enough years had passed, during which some of the officials had died or otherwise left office, men other than the Islanders were elected to office. A third violation was that all officials were supposed to be able to write. Of all the Islanders, only Francisco de Arocha could write a fair hand, and he was appointed secretary of the *cabildo*.[12]

This group of Canary Islanders was originally intended to be only the first of several groups of immigrants, but bringing them across the Atlantic had proved to be so expensive that further such plans were abandoned. The community stayed small for many years, and it faced continual problems. Indian raids; strife among the original settlers, missionaries, and the Islanders; power struggles among the Islanders themselves; and severe weather conditions made farming unpredictable, all contributing to the poverty of the settlement.[13]

The colonial government in Mexico City appointed José de Urrutia to be captain of the presidio in 1733. Under his leadership, retaliatory raids against the Apaches resulted in the capture of many Indian hostages, and the fate of these hostages provoked more quarrels between missionaries and presidials. Additionally, disputes arose between the missionaries and the Islanders over the use of mission Indian labor, crop damage to the settlers' farms from mission cattle, water rights, and more. The Islanders were very proud of being hidalgos, and their assumption of aristocratic postures did not ease tensions between them and the older inhabitants of Béxar.[14]

Part of the Islanders' attitudes arose from the legacies of the Reconquest. From that time, the only occupations that a gentleman could enjoy were military careers and ranching, because those could be done on horseback. Islanders felt that it was beneath their status as hidalgos to work with their hands or farm. Those jobs belonged to peasants, not to nobility, and while they had been peasants in the not-too-distant past, they were now hidalgos. There was also the human-nature component—the farmers wanted to expand their land and profit as much as possible. The Islanders, who were mainly farming people, demanded that the mission fathers and civilian ranchers fence their cattle spreads to prevent damage to the Islanders' crops. The fathers and ranchers responded by urging the Islanders to fence their crops instead. Disputes of this nature went on for years. The ill feeling between these groups was aggravated by the fact that there was not enough food for the settlers, while the mission had excess cattle. Since the cattle ran wild, Islanders would prey on the herds at night. Initially, the missionaries did not mind the settlers taking a few of the excess cattle; however, they did protest when the raids turned into wanton, wholesale slaughter.[15]

As time passed, the community began to come together. In 1750 the population was about five hundred, and by the mid-

1770s it had grown to 1,350. Facing mutual enemies like the Apaches forced the inhabitants of villa, presidio, and mission to work together. Compromises on the issues of cattle and crops eased the stress between different groups. Intermarriage and godfather relationships (*compadrazgo*) brought families closer. Beginning with the first generation of Islanders, intermarriage with non-Islanders increased, so that by the fourth generation no person could claim pure Canary Islander descent. As the original members of the city council retired, their places were filled by non-Islanders. By the late 1740s, the forty-five families who were not Islanders, and who had a generation earlier chafed under the rule of the arrogant minority, started to come into power themselves. San Fernando, both by intermarriage and the institution of Spanish laws that encouraged and protected the community, thus evolved into a cohesive whole.[16]

As the inspection of Pedro de Rivera in the late 1720s led to the settlement of the Islanders, the frontier inspection of the Marqués de Rubí in 1767 likewise led to significant changes for Texas. Rubí was not happy with the conditions of the presidios in Texas. He recommended that crumbling, useless military structures be abandoned and that missions without Indian converts be closed. He further recommended that the missions in East Texas be closed and the people sent to San Antonio, which would be designated the new capital. As with nearly all other cases, the Spanish bureaucracy moved very slowly before accepting Rivera's report. His recommendations were put into effect only partially in 1771, and not until 1773 was San Antonio designated the capital of Texas.[17]

★ 6 ★

Women's Status in Case Law from San Fernando de Béxar

THE PEOPLE OF San Fernando did not prosper quickly. A description of the community in 1740 mentioned wretched huts, called *jacales,* as living quarters for most of the settlers, though some had built stone shelters. No public buildings had been erected because there was no time for anything other than trying to survive on the harsh frontier. There was no surplus food, generally regarded as a requisite for civilization, and little or no education among the populace. In short, this was an exceedingly poor community, situated on the outlying fringe of European civilization. It was barely surviving, but it was Spanish. The populace, therefore, found the time and energy to sue each other.[1]

The Spanish were not only litigious but also quite diligent in their record-keeping. All official events, including lawsuits, were recorded in detail. The surviving documents from San Antonio de Béxar are contained in the Béxar Archives. Though women were a part of the San Fernando community from its founding in 1718, there is no case law recorded in the Béxar

Archives regarding women until 1735, four years after the Canary Islanders arrived. A study of this case law suggests that Spanish women on the frontier enjoyed all the privileges and protections established by the *Partidas* and the *Recopilación*. The legal capacity of women is partially substantiated by their ability to grant power of attorney to those who conducted business for them in far-away places. Women could buy and sell both personal and real property on their own; they could also be held and hold others to their contracts. Further, they could be held liable for their actions, both civil and criminal. Women were witnesses in civil and criminal trials, and their testimony carried just as much weight as that of men. These women made wills and were executors of wills. In short, the Spanish legal system translated well to the frontier situation with little modification of the traditional rights enjoyed by women in Spain or in the more settled regions of New Spain.

There were few, if any, lawyers on the Spanish frontier—apparently none in Texas—so it was the custom for people who had to transact business in a far-distant place to appoint a friend, relative, or well-known businessman to protect their interests there. This grant of the power of attorney was used by both men and women, although usually only men received such powers. Power of attorney was made by following a form, as is evident from the fact that the wording of all such grants is almost identical. Women apparently granted this power often enough that special wording was incorporated into the form when it was conferred by them. This extra wording included the renunciation by the woman of all special protections due her by law because of her sex. In essence, she had entered the man's world of business and agreed to be as responsible as a man for her actions, and she could not claim later that she did not know what she was doing.

Most of the grants of power of attorney in the Béxar Archives were made by widows. In 1743 doña Rosa Flores y Valdés, widow of Captain don Joseph de Urrutia, and her children gave power of attorney to don Juan de Angulo of Mexico City to settle the affairs of the deceased. Don Angulo must not have done a very good job, because in 1745 doña Rosa revoked that grant and gave power of attorney to don Joseph de Plazas of Boca de Leones to settle their claims. In both cases, she renounced all laws that favored women. Another widow, doña Josepha Flores y Valdés, gave power of attorney to don Francisco de Liñán to settle the estates of both of her deceased husbands, since both died intestate. She also renounced all laws in favor of women.[2]

Married women could also grant power of attorney. In 1770 Raphaela de la Garza gave power of attorney to her new husband, Francisco Flores de Abrego, to act on her behalf. This action would have been impossible under English common law, since that legal system assumed that the husband had total control over all his wife's property. Under Spanish law, the wife had to swear that she was not compelled, persuaded, or forced to give this power to her husband but did so of her own free will. This one-page document demonstrates that Spanish married women had control over their own property, that they did not have to give it up to their husbands, and that furthermore it was uncommon for them to do so. It also shows that married women did sometimes grant this power to their husbands, because there was a standard form for such a transaction.[3]

Brothers and sisters could join in granting power of attorney. In 1744 don Francisco Maldonado, doña María Maldonado, Luis Maldonado, and Juana Francisca Treviño gave power of attorney to their uncle in Saltillo to settle claims regarding land inherited from their mutual grandfather. Again, the use of a form is evident. This one reads, "The said women grantors renounce the laws relative to and in favor of women in order that they may be compelled to comply" with a possible future court order.[4]

Women had to renounce laws in their favor in order to buy and sell property. The only instances in the Béxar Archives of personal property being sold under a contract are formal agreements for the sale of slaves. Black slavery was common throughout New Spain, but it was relatively scarce on the frontier, probably because of the poverty of the inhabitants. The ownership of slaves was regulated, as was every part of Spanish life. In slave sales, the ownership history of the slave had to be of public record to establish that this person was a previously owned slave. For example, in 1743 doña Josepha Flores y Valdés[5] sold her slave, Luis, to Lt. Colonel don Justo Boneo y Morales, the governor and captain general of Texas. The document includes the information that she had received the slave from her late husband, don Miguel Núñez Morillo, and that the sale was for two hundred pesos cash. At the same time, Boneo y Morales sold to doña Josepha Flores y Valdés a slave named Francisco Joseph, whom he got from doña María Eugenia de Oliva, wife of a Spaniard living in Mexico City. The price of this slave was 270 pesos in cash.[6]

Women could not only buy and sell slaves, they could, if they were of African descent, also be slaves. Slaves, of course, had very few rights. The female slave María de los Dolores was bought from doña María Fernández de Castro. This document does not list the name of the buyer, nor the sale price. It seems that only the ownership history needed to be recorded. A more complex case was that of María Gertrudis de la Peña, an Indian native of Camargo. She was owned by two men before being sold to don Angel Navarro. María Gertrudis claimed that she was supposed to have been regarded as a daughter to her first owner but became pregnant by him when she was sixteen. She was then sold to her second owner, supposedly to be treated as a daughter, not as a slave. She was happy there until her owner got angry at her and took away all her clothes. Her testimony stated that Navarro promised her that if he bought her and she worked for him for three years he would free her. She agreed to this arrangement, but after entering his household, she believed that he treated her badly, so she brought suit against him to be freed immediately.[7]

Since Spanish law specified that Indians could not be enslaved, the judge, Governor Domingo Cabello, declared María free and not bound in any way to Navarro. The court advised her to return to her own people. By Spanish law Indians had most of the rights of Spanish people, and the laws protecting Spanish women extended to cover Indian women as well. If María had grown up in a Spanish community, she would have been familiar with her rights and known that she could not be enslaved. The court also seems to have taken the facts into account and used the laws that brought the most justice to the plaintiff. Spanish officials appear to have been very protective of helpless women, even if the woman was an Indian.[8]

There was no question that women, married or widowed, could own land. One of the inducements for people to move to San Fernando was free land: a person simply had to petition the *cabildo* for a lot and live on it, or otherwise improve it, to own it in fee simple. Usually the husband, as head of the household, would make the petition and hold title to the land, but this was not always the case. In 1745 Tomasa de la Garza, describing herself as a *vecina agregada,* or a settler who had been added to the community, petitioned on behalf of her husband, Gabriel de los Ríos, for a lot on which to live. In the petition, she cited the fact that their eight children, including one widow, lived with them. *She* was granted title; *she* performed the acts of possession. *She* "dug in the ground, threw earth, pulled up the stakes, marked the boundaries, and performed all the other ceremonies necessary according to law, as the legitimate owner, holder, and possessor of the said town lot."[9]

Once the petitioner had lived on the lot long enough to have clear title, the land could be sold. Again, there is absolutely no question that women could buy and sell real property, provided that they renounced all laws in favor of women. In 1746 doña Juana de Urrutia, widow of don Ygnacio González, sold land to don Diego Ramón. The lot was described as fifty *varas* square, fenced with a board fence on two sides, with sixteen peach trees and a house with all its improvements. The price was five hundred pesos. The deed followed the same form as all deeds executed by men, except that it included the now familiar clause that doña Juana renounced all laws favorable to women.[10]

The hazards of life on the frontier, especially for young men, led to widowhood for many women. Many of the women selling land were widows, and this status was so stated in the deed. Much of the time the marital status does not seem to have been included for any legal purpose, but merely to identify the woman more precisely. Gertrudis de la Garza, widow of Martín Saucedo, sold to don Alberto López a lot with fruit trees on it. In this case, the husband had contracted the sale before his death, and his widow was completing the transaction. She still had to renounce all laws in favor of women. Gabriela de los Ríos sold Juan Joseph Villegas a fenced lot on the *acequia* for one hundred pesos. No mention was made of her marital status. Doña Josepha Flores y Valdés bought land near the presidio from Joseph de Montemayor for fifty pesos. No mention was made of her marital status, either, but in other places she was listed as a widow.[11]

A husband could not sell land belonging to the married couple without the consent of the wife. Don Manuel de Niza, with the express permission of his wife, doña Sebastiana de la Peña, sold land to don Thoribio de Urrutia in 1748. "We" was used throughout the deed of sale, and in addition to renouncing all laws in favor of women, doña Sebastiana separately averred that she was not intimidated by her husband.[12]

Normally, the husband would represent his wife's legal interests. In 1770 don Francisco Caravajal brought suit on behalf of his wife, doña María, to regain land. The first owner of the lot, Mateo de Caravajal, grandfather of María, had received it from the Crown. Mateo built a house on the lot and lived there. One of the town's mayors gave part of this land to two brothers, Andrés and Francisco Hernández. Andrés sold his portion to his niece, doña Josepha Hernández, and Francisco sold part of his parcel to Joseph Caravajal, son of Mateo, who should have had all the land by right of inheritance.

As part of this suit, Josepha Hernández claimed that she did own part of the land and that the title was in the town's archives. Doña Josepha signed her own name to this document. One of the witnesses, doña Juana de Oyos, was also supposed to have signed her own name, but there is no such mark in the translation. This degree of literacy was very unusual in San Fernando, for most people simply made a mark, and the scribe wrote in their names. The first decision was in favor of don Francisco, "husband and conjoint person of" his wife, María.

The decision as to the exact limits of the property was disputed by the defendant, doña Josepha Hernández. The eventual outcome of the suit was that the land was recognized as belonging to doña María de Caravajal. The major peace officer gave possession to doña María in the presence of doña Josepha, and doña María walked the boundaries. So even though the suit was brought by the husband, the land belonged to the wife.[13]

A married woman did face some constraints on her ability to buy and sell real property. In a suit brought in 1771, Ygnacia de Castro sought to void a contract to sell her property to her brother, because he had not made any payments beyond the down payment. Her argument was based on the lack of a written deed, and she claimed he had acted maliciously in trying to defraud her of her land. Ygnacia's brother, Marcos de Castro, claimed that since Ygnacia was married at the time of the contract, she could not enforce it. The court held that the plaintiff's marital status was "irrelevant" because the defendant had indeed acted maliciously. The contract was voided and Ygnacia retained her land.[14]

Women often exercised their rights to sue for damages. Magdalena Leal owned a reed field that was damaged by Vicente Amador's horse. Vicente belied his surname when he attacked the deputy who told him to retrieve his mare and pay the damages. María de Caravajal, as part of the suit mentioned previously to regain her land from the Hernández family, brought suit on her own for damages resulting from the defendant's use of the land during the lawsuit. Doña Josepha Hernández answered the order to stop building on the land until the settlement of the suit by asking that it be dropped. She claimed that the land was hers and she could build on it if she wanted. As noted above, María was given possession of the land in the presence of Josepha, probably to forestall any further claims of encroachment.[15]

Although Spanish law, as well as Spanish men enforcing it, favored women, this did not mean that women won every lawsuit that they brought against men. María Eugencia Rodríguez, a widow, sued to retain land that she claimed had been granted to her husband and was being requested by don Domingo Delgado. She wanted her title ratified so that he could not seize her improved land and force her onto the unimproved portion. Witnesses were called to testify as to the original grant to her husband, and they all agreed that what she was claiming was not part of the original grant. The court ruled that she had no title to the land, and the municipal council granted the land to Delgado.[16]

One of the earliest suits in the Béxar Archives was filed by Antonia Lusgardia Hernández. She petitioned governor and captain general don Miguel de Sandoval for the return of her son from don Miguel Núñez. She had been working for don Miguel for eight or nine years for no salary and had left because of poor treatment and because he would not give her any clothes. She had a daughter before she went into service and had a son while she was there. When she left, she claimed that don Miguel took away her son, "the only man I have and the one who I hope will eventually support me." She threw herself on the mercy of the court: "I being but a poor helpless woman whose only protection is a good administration and a good legal system." Although she could not name them, she asked for the protection of all laws in her favor.[17]

Don Sandoval, no doubt proud that being the good administrator of a good legal system enabled him to help this poor woman, ordered the boy returned. Don Miguel agreed to comply with the order, but he replied that the boy Ignacio had left his mother of his own free will in order to be with his godmother, doña Josepha Flores, who happened to be the wife of don Miguel. Don Miguel claimed that Antonia gave the boy to doña Josepha and renounced all her rights to him, so she should not get him back. Don Miguel also claimed that he wanted merely to protect the boy, who had a good, spiritual relationship with his godmother.[18]

This case does point out the value that the Spanish placed on family, whether as a support for a "poor helpless woman" or as a godson. Nowhere was the parentage of the boy asked. Apparently, the identity of the father was not important to the disposition of the case. This case also shows that even a very poor woman knew her legal rights and was not afraid to go to court to enforce them. Spanish women living on such an isolated frontier must have passed on the knowledge of their rights from mother to daughter and between friends.

Not every familial relationship was so loving, especially when property was involved. Raphaela de la Garza brought suit against her own son, Joseph Antonio Curbelo. She stated that he had come into her house claiming that because she had remarried, her new husband should provide her a new house and that they should leave this one, which had been his father's, to him. The son then tried to kill the second husband with a sword. The son counter-claimed that his mother and her second husband had tried to put him out of his own house. For that reason, he armed himself with the sword. He also asked for his father's will to be probated so his stepfather would not spend all his inheritance. The outcome of this case is not contained in the archives.[19]

Since women had every right to dispose of their own property, they also had the right to use wills to dispose of property after their death. The earliest woman's will and testament found in the Béxar Archives is that of María Melián. Her will, dated December 3, 1740, was typical of Spanish wills of that period. She first directed that two *reales* (coins worth 1/8 peso) be donated to the Holy Church of Jerusalem to ransom captives and help orphaned girls. Doña María had been married twice, and she stated that the only property that had been brought into the second marriage was one cow, which had given birth to four offspring during her second marriage. One of this cow's offspring was to be given to the youngest daughter, and one given to her son from her first marriage. Her other children were to be given cows from the five she had received for settling in San Fernando. All the rest of her property was to be divided equally among her children from both marriages.[20]

This will sheds light on several aspects of property ownership under Spanish law. The gift to the Church came first, before any other property was distributed. Next, she divided her property into what was hers by right of settlement and what came to her in each of her marriages. A Spanish marriage was ganancial in nature—meaning that the people entering into it expected to make material gains during the marriage and that these gains would be the result of both their efforts. Therefore, any gains accruing during the marriage would be split evenly between the marital partners. The one cow that she brought into the second marriage was her own personal property. Its offspring during the marriage would be divided equally between her and her husband; therefore, she devised two of the four offspring to two of her children. The one given to her youngest daughter was probably intended to form part of her dowry, and the one given to her eldest son may have been motivated by the fact that he would not inherit from her second husband, or it may be simply because he was her eldest child.[21]

There was no differentiation between male and female offspring in the division of the remainder of her estate: all her children shared equally. This lack of prejudice against females was very different from what would have been the case under English common law, where males, especially the firstborn son, would have received the bulk of the estate. Men and women were both vital to the survival of the community on the Spanish frontier, and Spanish wills demonstrate this.

The will of Mateo Pérez, though undated, was probably written in 1746 or 1747. Don Mateo was apparently a wealthy man by San Fernando standards. The first several items in his will were a list of debts owed to him by various people. Gertrudis de la Cruz, wife of Joseph Lizardo, owed him sixteen pesos for material. Note that she, not her husband, owed him, even though the husband's name is used for identification purposes. This case nicely illustrates that married women were responsible for their own debts. Dominga (no last name) owed Mateo eight pesos, four *reales*. Gertrudis, widow of Joseph de Sosa, owed him twelve pesos. Ana García (marital status not mentioned) owed him six pesos in corn.[22]

After listing the debts, Mateo explained that his sons had already been given horses, so he bequeathed an equivalent amount of money to his daughter, María Antonia. This practice was very common. Sons and daughters would receive their expectancy during the parent's life, and it would be deducted from what they received through the will. In this case, Mateo's sons had each been given a horse as part of their expectancy, so the daughter received the value of a horse in cash from the estate in order that all would inherit equally.[23]

Family was very important to the Spanish, regardless of legitimacy and regardless of actual parentage. Mateo bequeathed the same amount of money to Rosa Pérez, a mestiza (part Spanish and part Indian) who was born in his house and raised as his daughter, and he also left her six breeding cows. Rosa's son Joseph María received two breeding cows, two horses, and a saddle. Even the servant, who was not considered part of the family, María de Zaragoza, received six cows and a bull. The legitimate children, not including Rosa, shared equally in the bulk of the estate. This distribution shows that Mateo wanted all his family to benefit from his estate, and to do so as equitably as possible. Bequests to illegitimate children and non–family members were made explicitly, as otherwise those people would not share in the estate. In this will, horses were given only to men, while cows were given to both men and women. The bulk of the estate was divided equally between Mateo's legitimate sons and daughters.[24]

The contrast between this disposition and one that would have been made under English common law is immense. Under English law, Mateo's eldest son would have inherited almost all of the estate. Younger sons would have received small portions, and the legitimate daughter might have received a portion as her dowry. Most likely, the illegitimate children and servant would not have been included at all. English common law will be discussed more completely in the next chapter.

Sometimes, of course, the distribution of property through a will did not happen amicably. Suits to force distribution of estates and to challenge distribution of estates were common in San Fernando. One fairly simple suit was that by a widow to prove she was the only heir of her husband. His will stated that she was his lawful wife and that their children would be his heirs after her death. In other words, he left her a life estate in his share of the community property. His will stated that all he owned was gained through the marriage, so he had no separate property to divide. That this suit was brought at all implies that the children did not want to wait for the death of their mother to receive their share of their father's estate.[25]

Suits would also be filed to settle the estate where the person died intestate. In 1771 Matías Guerra filed a suit against Juan Ignacio Guerra to divide their father's estate. Cayetano Guerra had not left a will, so his legitimate daughters, Rosalia, Bernarda, and Antonia, and his legitimate sons, Matías and Juan, split the bulk of the estate equally. Special bequests, in the form of silk shirts, were given to Cayetano's two illegitimate daughters. All interested parties attested that they were agreeable to the division, with husbands signing for their wives. Again, family was important. Even illegitimate daughters shared in the estate.[26]

When there was no will and land was involved in the deceased's estate, a suit could be filed to determine the eventual disposition of the land. Such an amicable suit to settle land ownership was filed so that mutual heirs would be able to sell land to a third party. Here a copy of the entire proceeding was given to the eldest sister so that the family would have a record and not bring any more suits.[27]

The criminal cases in the Béxar Archives do not often involve women. When women were part of a criminal trial, it was usually as witnesses. For example, when Quiteria Múzquiz was called as a witness in the murder trial of the Indian Andrés, she took the same oath as the male witnesses and her testimony held the same weight as theirs. Even the Indian wife of Andrés was sworn in through an interpreter and allowed to give her testimony.[28]

The record of the one criminal case during this period where a woman was imprisoned tells of murder and adultery. It is very enlightening about the change in Spanish attitudes toward these crimes on the frontier. Juan de Sosa was accused of murdering Diego Menchaca. Sosa confessed to the deed but claimed he did it because Menchaca was committing adultery with his (Sosa's) wife. Under Spanish law, this would be a complete defense to the charge of murder, but the wife would then be held guilty of adultery. Therefore, when Juan made this defense, his wife, Gertrudis Barrón, was arrested, shackled, and imprisoned. However, the charge brought against her was not adultery but that her actions had led to the murder of Diego and that she was therefore responsible for his death. Juan de Sosa was set free when it was determined that he did, in fact, act to defend his wife's honor. Gertrudis was also freed, and no charge of adultery was ever brought against her. Apparently, as in Castile, if Juan could forgive his wife, so could the law.[29]

This case law illustrates that the traditional Spanish law as embodied in the *Partidas* survived the transition to the frontier mostly intact. That should not be surprising, since the ideas of the *Partidas* developed on the frontier of the Reconquest. Spanish women knew their rights. They knew that they could own property; that they could buy it, sell it, inherit it, and be responsible for it. On the frontier this ability of women to handle their own affairs was important, since the men were so often away fighting Indians or on other business.

★ 7 ★

The Impact of English History on the Development of English Common Law

Much as the history of Spain had a great impact on the development of Castilian law, the history of England shaped the development of the English common law. The written history of England begins with the Roman occupation in the first century of the current era. But even more than was the case in Spain, the Romans left no perceptible impact on the society or legal systems of the British Isles. By the end of the Roman era in the fourth century, all that remained of the Roman presence were the physical structures such as roads, bridges, baths, and especially Hadrian's Wall. Very few documents survived. The first group of conquerors who left an indelible mark on Britain's social and legal systems were the Angles and Saxons coming across the English Channel from Germany. The Anglo-Saxons ruled England from about 450 to 1066, and it was from their legal system that the common law first developed. The early Anglo-Saxons formed a loose confederation in England with many leaders of the various groups. Tribal leaders were generally warlords in times of war and community leaders in times of peace. Even during the few times that the Anglo-Saxons fought under one king, that king took advice from all the other leaders. Successful warlords would seize land from other groups and add it to their own territory, thus increasing the size of the kingdoms in England while reducing their overall number. By the seventh century, there were only seven kingdoms; these gradually merged into three, Northumbria, Mercia, and Wessex,

The British Isles in Anglo-Saxon times.

which acted together in times of duress. The Anglo-Saxon kingdoms had unified under one ruler just in time to be conquered by the Normans in 1066.[1]

The various leaders of Anglo-Saxon England ruled by virtue of their personalities and accomplishments, and their subjects obeyed commands out of a sense of personal loyalty. Early Anglo-Saxon leaders were more warlord or chieftain than the present-day definition of king, but for the sake of simplicity, this work will refer to them as kings. The king was responsible for the whole of his people, and his people were responsible to him. Over time, the king added to his personal power by displays of wealth and royalty. Wearing a crown, sitting on a raised throne, and receiving the homages of his subjects all separated the king from the rest of the leaders. Once the king became more than a warlord, he had the obligation to rule his kingdom well. He became responsible for punishing criminals who violated the king's peace and for delivering justice to his subjects. Most punishments, for crimes and civil remedies, were in the form of fines paid to either the injured party or the king, or both. Some crimes that the king deemed to be destructive of society could not be remedied by fine, only by capital punishment. These crimes eventually transmuted into felonies, and crimes that could be remedied by fines became misdemeanors in United States jurisdictions.[2]

There were several classes and classifications of men in Anglo-Saxon society, and historians continue to disagree on exactly what each encompassed. One category of man was the ceorl. Sometimes this class label defined unfree persons bound to the land; sometimes it described a free agricultural tenant; sometimes it meant a wealthy landowner. A person's class could be determined by the amount of his or her wergeld (also spelled *wergild*). When a malefactor killed an innocent person, the offender had to pay a fine called the wergeld. This compensation was paid to the victim's kin. The higher a person's status was, the higher his or her wergeld was. A ceorl's wergeld was usually set at two hundred shillings. A thegn's wergeld might be 1,200 shillings, but historians' descriptions of a thegn vary from a servant boy to a baron. The difference between free and unfree likewise is unclear. A man might be technically free but still owe such duties to his lord that he was unable to exercise that freedom. A man who was technically bound to the land might be owed service by a freeman.[3]

The king was usually the best warrior, and his men followed him because they thought he could best protect them and their rights. The society was a mixture of free and unfree, with all persons owing obligations of some sort to other persons. The king was at the top, and various strata of nobility descended toward the bottom. The king, or lord, granted rights to his followers. In return, the followers were loyal to the king. The king protected his people, and in return the people owed military service to the king. So there was a bond of mutual obligations between the lord and his men. The king, however, was not yet divine. His right to rule came from a contract with his subjects. He had special privileges, such as higher recompense for wrongs done to him, but he was not above the law. The king's wergeld was also set so high that no one would contemplate killing him, because to do so would bankrupt the malefactor's family and they would all be sold into slavery to pay the debt. Nonlethal crimes could be compensated by the mundbyrd, a fine levied to compensate for an injury to person or property. The amount of the fine varied with the status of the injured party.[4]

The nobility, whether thegns, ceorls, or barons, owed much

The Impact of English History on English Common Law   91

the same duties to the people sworn to them as the king owed to the nobles. The nobles collected duties, taxes, fines, and military service from their men and paid those same debts to the king. The reality of each noble's duties and rights varied because each came from a personal contract with the king. The nobles who were closer personally to the king usually got more rights and fewer duties than those who were out of favor or far away. All nobles had the right and duty to keep the peace within their realms. They settled disputes and dispensed justice in their lands much as the king did for the whole kingdom.[5]

Local justice may have been pronounced by the local lord in court, but in reality it was enforced by the men of the area. These people all knew each other, knew the value of each man's wergeld and mundbyrd, and knew the character of each of their neighbors. Most freemen were subsistence farmers; few commercial transactions took place. In an illiterate society, transactions that did occur had to be witnessed to be valid. For example, when a man went to another town to buy a cow, he would first announce his intention to his neighbors. In the town where the transaction took place, the men of the area would witness the sale so that all would know the sale was legitimate. When he returned, he would show the new cow to the same men in his hometown so that all knew the cow was his. If the purchase was not planned ahead, the buyer would put his new cow in the common pasture for all to see and announce it was his. The common memory of all who witnessed the transaction would form the basis of testimony in court, should that be necessary.[6]

Of all the crimes mentioned in the various dooms, or laws, rules concerning theft and the apprehension of thieves are almost double that of any other crime. The next most numerous laws deal with assault and killing. All honest men had the duty to apprehend offenders and had to pay a fine if they let the suspect escape. The only defense would be to prove that they did not know that the person involved was a criminal. The prevalence of laws on theft shows the importance of property to the Anglo-Saxons, and the fact that all crimes could be punished by fines emphasizes that the thrust of the law was on the protection of property. The fact that the fines were paid to the injured party demonstrates that the penalties were private compensation for wrongs done to a person. Later, crimes would be seen as being offenses against society, and punishments would be for the public benefit.[7]

One aspect of Anglo-Saxon law that did not carry over into the Norman era concerned the relationship of husband and wife. Spouses were not considered to be related to each other. This fact is shown in the wergelds. As mentioned, wergelds were the price to be paid when a person was killed, which would be paid to the deceased's kindred. Kindred was extremely important to that society and feuds often started from avenging a wrong done to some kin. When a wife was killed, her wergeld went to her birth family, not to her husband. If a husband killed his wife, he too had to pay her wergeld to her kin. If a wife committed a crime, her kin, not her husband, had to pay her fine. This Germanic tradition did not give ownership of the wife to her husband. Instead, even in marriage she remained her own person with her own rights, privileges, and responsibilities. In Spain, this concept evolved into the ideas of separate property and continuing separate identity of a married woman. In England, this attitude that wives did not belong to their husbands changed with the advent of Christianity in England and became law with the institution of Norman legal practices after the conquest.[8]

As the status of a man determined the fine due when he was injured, so a woman's status determined the fine due her for an injury. The dooms of Alfred, king of Wessex from 871 to 899, list numerous fines for various injuries. A man who stole a woman out of a nunnery, for example, had to pay 120 shillings. This was the equivalent of twenty oxen: quite a high price and generally impossible for most people to pay. A man who committed adultery with another man's wife had to pay the wronged husband one-tenth the amount of his wergeld. On the other hand, a man who kidnapped a common woman owed only five shillings. If he took her virginity, he had to pay another sixty shillings, but if she was not a virgin, the fine for rape was reduced to thirty shillings, or the cost of five oxen. This fine was still beyond the ability of most men to pay. Alfred intended his dooms to prevent crimes by making the fines prohibitively high. The imposition of such high fines for rape suggests that the Anglo-Saxons valued their women more than did other nations of Europe, which punished rape lightly or not at all.[9]

Anglo-Saxon women also took part in lawsuits, both as litigants and as oath helpers. About 990 C.E., Wynflaed, a noblewoman, sued Leofwine for possession of land. King Ethlered the Redeless heard the case. Wynflaed claimed that she received the estates of Hagbournes and Bradfield, and she produced some very high-ranking oath helpers to back her up. The archbishop of Canterbury, another bishop, and, perhaps most convincing to the king, his own mother, swore that Wynflaed was telling the truth. Wynflaed also produced thirty-six witnesses to the transaction who were willing to swear for her. The king, convinced by the preponderance of the oath helpers, awarded the land to Wynflaed.[10]

In a case during the reign of King Canute, a shire court

heard another case involving a woman's ownership of property. Edwin sued his mother, Enneawnes, for two estates. None of the court knew the particulars of the case, so they asked for witnesses. The people who knew most about the case were the kin of Edwin and Enneawnes. Thurkel the White, husband of Enneawnes's kinswoman Leofflaed, stood up for Enneawnes but could not swear that he had witnessed any transactions. Therefore, the court ordered him and three thegns to ride to Enneawnes and find out what happened. Enneawnes swore to them that she had never given her son Edwin any of her land, but that she had given it to Leofflaed, her kinswoman. The thegns were convinced, and the court awarded the land to Leofflaed. Here is a case, then, of a woman (Enneawnes), marital status unknown, selling land to a married woman (Leofflaed). The role of Thurkel the White, husband of the eventual landowner, was only that of witness: none of the land belonged to him.[11]

Inheritance laws also followed Germanic custom. A man usually left the bulk of his land to his eldest son, with personal property going to his daughters; but if he had no sons, his daughters inherited the land. Few records remain on marriage cases from that era. Most cases concerned the disposition of marriage gifts where the wife had died before bearing children. Anglo-Saxon women, married, single, or widowed, had complete ability to own, buy, and sell land. They could also dispose of it in wills, the same as men. That would change with the Norman Conquest.[12]

The Normans ruled England only from 1066 to 1154, but they left an indelible mark on the society and its legal system. The Norman rulers were William the Conqueror (1066–1087), his sons William Rufus (1087–1100) and Henry I (1100–1135), and the chaotic rules of Stephen, Matilda, and the years of anarchy (1135–1154). The Norman concept of kingship was more developed than that of the Anglo-Saxons had been. Where the Anglo-Saxon kings ruled by personal charisma and ability, Normans ruled by divine right. Normans imposed their institutions on England, especially the system of vassalage.[13]

The Norman kings ruled absolutely. Though they had advisors, they did not have to follow their advice. The Normans brought the concept of divine-right kingship to England. They wanted their government to be strong and their subjects to be obedient. The Normans retained those parts of the Anglo-Saxon government that they found useful, but made them more efficient. Fines imposed for violations of the king's justice and fees paid by vassals for certain privileges all came into the king's treasury. As the king's need for money increased, so did the fines and fees.[14]

The Angevins, who ruled England from 1154 to 1216, also placed high emphasis on a strong king and the complete obedience of the subject. Henry II, who ruled from 1154 to 1189, was one of England's most accomplished kings and definitely the greatest of all the medieval English kings. He brought peace to the land and efficiency to his government. His son Richard the Lion-Hearted is more famous, but actually he was an inept ruler. Richard's interest in personal glory and the Crusades far outweighed his interest in the backwater country of England. Although he ruled for only ten years, he managed to bankrupt the country with his incessant need of money to finance his military exploits. His brother John is also one of the more famous, or infamous, English kings. His attempts to wring more taxes out of the barons to send to Richard, and his unwillingness to compromise even after Richard's death in 1199, ended with his barons forcing him to sign the Magna Carta in 1215. Civil war soon followed, and in 1216 John died. He was followed by his young son, who became Henry III.[15]

Henry II is usually regarded as the founder of English common law. He began with the customary law and procedure already in place and used his royal prerogative to mold it into a complete legal system. These changes came not from legislation but from administration; few laws were passed during his reign, but administrative orders changed the judicial procedure, organization of the courts, and even the substance of the laws. Henry II's reign corresponded with the rise of universities and the revival of Roman law, and he surrounded himself with educated advisors. His own motives, however, were not simply to spread justice throughout his kingdom. Henry was more interested in the accumulation of income to his treasury.[16]

Legal procedure changed during Henry's reign. The jury under Anglo-Saxon law was a group of freemen who knew the parties and the facts of the suit. They judged the outcome of the trials by combat and by ordeal. Under the Normans, these bodies continued to be an evidence-giving group. Under the Angevins, the jury became a truth-finding body; it heard the evidence and declared who was telling the truth. Jury trials became the accepted practice under Henry II. The other major change in the legal procedure was the grand assize, instituted by Henry II. Under this rule, a defendant could decline trial by combat or ordeal and have a jury hear evidence to decide the case. In criminal cases, too, grand jury indictments and jury trials became common. The rationality of this type of court procedure quickly overcame the traditional methods of ordeal and combat, although both remained in infrequent use until the nineteenth century.[17]

The next English king who concentrated his efforts on the legal system was Edward I (1272–1307). He focused on improving the financial condition of the kingdom by increasing the tax base. The early royal household position of the wardrobe developed from a simple clerical post into a mighty treasury. This unofficial treasury department, unlike the official exchequer, was not under the control of the barons. It was used by the king as a war chest and supply center for his military. The official taxes grew, as well. New taxes on personal property soon exceeded the old fees of scutage (a tax paid in lieu of military service), tallage (a tax on royal towns and lands), and carucage (a tax on plow). Edward also instituted a customs tax on wool. All these taxes, however, had to be obtained by the consent of the taxed, and this would lay a great foundation for the British parliament.[18]

The thirteenth century saw the codification of the majority of the English common law. Edward I's numerous statutes regularized and systematized the complex and contradictory laws from various parts of the realm. The common law of England included the royal prerogative, the statutory law, and the common law, or "that which has always been law." It did not include special laws for specific and unusual circumstances. Most of the common law developed at the hands of royal judges as they heard cases throughout England. Judges could follow precedent or establish new rulings; during the reign of Henry III they often established new remedies, and so created new laws. Almost all of these judges were well educated, being knowledgeable in canon and Roman law as well as common law. The most famous lawyer and judge of medieval England was Henry de Bracton, who wrote *Concerning the Laws and Customs of England* in the 1250s. He emphasized that the law should follow precedent: namely, that a case should be decided based on how previous cases like it had been resolved. He declared that the law made the king, not vice versa. Bracton also emphasized intent as a necessary component of any misdeed. Bracton's work became the basis for the common law until replaced by Sir William Blackstone in the eighteenth century.[19]

The system of vassalage that came from the Normans assumed that all land was in service to the king. The theory was that he gave his vassals the possession and use of some of his land in return for their service—usually military service. The rights of ownership were often called seizen, because the person "was seized of" the land. These rights varied between people and over times, and often existed in layers, so they are difficult to classify. When the vassal died, his heir could usually inherit the possession and usage of the land, if he paid a fee to the king. As the nobility increased their power, they persuaded the kings to give them more permanent grants of land. Unlike what happened in Spain, in England power and wealth came from the land itself, and the nobility wanted to keep their lands in their possession forever.[20]

The rule of primogeniture, where the eldest son inherited all the lands of the estate, came into use in England to protect the family powerbase. Younger sons could not inherit the lands of the father's estate. In 1285 the law *De donis conditionalibus* allowed the estate "tail," meaning ownership of the land was limited in some way. The most common form of this limitation was the entailed estate, in which only the eldest son could inherit. Usually, the ownership was limited to the heirs so that the estate would not be forfeited to the king upon the death of the vassal. The intention was to prohibit the sale of these lands and thereby ensure they would descend to the heirs. Lawyers gradually created means of getting around entail and allowing free alienation, or sale, of the land.[21] The concentration of power in land makes England's legal system very different from Spain's. In Spain during the centuries of the Reconquest, there was always enough land for everyone, so law did not develop for the purpose of protecting it, as happened in England. Entail and primogeniture did not have the force in Spain that they did in England. In Spain, the king never controlled all of the land; the nobles acquired their lands through their own conquests, so feudalism did not develop to the extent it did in England or France. The Spanish never held the ownership of land in as high esteem as did the English. The Spanish laws developed instead to protect the Spanish community.

One important concept that developed in England during this time was the idea that personal property could be separate from real property. Until the twelfth century, all personal property belonged with the real property to which it was attached. The landowner would bring suit for the recovery of a cow that had been misappropriated, and would be paid back with a cow. The use of cattle as a method of payment was so common that the word meaning cattle, "chattel," became the word to describe personal property. By the thirteenth century, compensation for damages became payments in cash instead of in kind.[22]

Inheritance laws had been codified in the reign of Edward I. Real property could not be disposed of in a will: it passed by feudal custom to the next tenant. Personal property, on the other hand, could be disposed of by will. If a man's wife survived but there were no children, she received half of the personal property. If the children survived but not the wife, then they received half of the property. In each case, the other half went to the Church as compensation for prayers on behalf of the deceased's soul. If both wife and children survived, each received one-third, with the rest to go to the Church. If the deceased left a will, the Church executed it according to canon law.[23]

During the fourteenth and fifteenth centuries, common law developed and became more elaborate without changing its essential nature. The rules of pleadings and procedure became tortuously complicated. Judges who had studied the law became the men who wrote the law, and they did it by delivering decisions based on precedent and pleadings. The common law became so highly structured that it was frequently impossible to achieve justice in its courts. Eventually the Courts of Chancery heard cases in equity, meaning they dispensed their opinions based on fairness, not complicated procedural issues. These chancery courts, however, were expensive and therefore their use was limited to the rich.[24]

Perhaps the best-known legal writer in all of Britain, William Blackstone made common law accessible to lawyers both in England and in its colonies in North America. He was born July 10, 1723, in London, to a merchant family. In 1741 Blackstone began his study of law in the Middle Temple; in 1744 he became a fellow of All Souls College at Oxford. He did not achieve fame by practicing law but by becoming a professor of it. Before his classes, the only law taught in universities was canon law. The lawyers-in-training learned common law by rote in the various Inns of Court in London. In these inns, public houses where they lived, students memorized cases and practiced arguing them until their peers decided they were ready to practice before the court. Blackstone changed this procedure. He lectured for years on English common law, then wrote his lectures down in four volumes entitled *Commentaries on the Laws of England*.[25]

In these four volumes, published in 1765, Blackstone reduced English common law to its essentials. By owning and reading this work, any reasonably intelligent man could begin to practice law in either England or America. Often, in America, this work was the only law book in a lawyer's office, or even in an entire city. Because his work was so easily understood and so practical, it became the common law as practiced in America. When states would adopt the common law of England, they meant they adopted the law as found in Blackstone's *Commentaries*.[26]

In *Commentaries*, women's legal status was defined clearly. It depended almost entirely on her marital status, because married women had very few rights. Blackstone declared that "the husband and wife are one person in law: that is, the very being or legal existence of the woman is suspended during the marriage." The husband could sell all of his wife's property without her consent, because everything she had belonged to him. A married woman could not make a will without her husband's consent, and even a widow could not make a will unless her husband had consented during his lifetime. A married woman's existence was "covered" by her lord and master: this is where the term *coverture* originated. During a woman's coverture, that is, during her marriage, she disappeared to the law, leaving her husband in total control of her person and her property. The adage most commonly quoted is that under English law, during the marriage, the husband and wife were one, and the husband was the one.[27]

Under English common law, a woman's marital status defined most of her civic rights. A single woman had almost the status of a man, but in practice few women remained single. A young woman's property would be handled by her father, and a spinster's property would usually be handled by some male member of her family. A widow had more freedom. She could handle her own affairs for the most part, but the tenet of common law controlled any property she inherited from her husband. Rich women had more freedom than poor ones, because under the equity courts a rich wife could set up a separate estate apart from her husband's influence. Chancery Courts, a separate institution from the regular court system, decided cases by equity rather than by the common law. They could either be a court of primary jurisdiction or a form of appeal, since England had no true appellate courts. A person who lost his or her case in the common-law courts could have the case retried in equity courts, which were not bound by common law but by justice. As noted, however, this process was very expensive. Taking a case to the Chancery Courts was usually for the protection of the woman's family's wealth rather than for the woman's own benefit.[28]

Unlike Spanish law where sons and daughters inherited equally, under English law only sons inherited real property. A husband owned all, not half, of the increase from a wife's separate property, and he could dispose of it as he wished, because all of her property became his upon marriage. A widower inherited all of a wife's estate, but a widow (assuming there were children) received a life estate in only one-third of the husband's real estate. This means that the inherited land, one-third of the land owned by her husband at his death, could not be sold during her lifetime. A wife could not bring suit in her own name except where the husband had absconded. A wife could not be sued without making the husband party to the suit, because she had no existence separate from him. A married woman could not make contracts, buy or sell land, or do business of any kind during her coverture. All such acts were void by law unless approved by the husband. Blackstone said that these laws were for the wife's protection because she was the favored sex in England. Eminent Virginia jurist St. George Tucker, who annotated the American version of *Blackstone's Commentaries* in 1803, indicated he would not equate "favored" with "discriminated against."[29]

Interpretation is, of course, a favorite occupation of both lawyers and historians. Whether society thought that women wanted or needed legal protection from their own actions depends on which society is indicated. Susan Staves points out in *Married Women's Separate Property in England, 1660–1833* that even such an apparently simple issue as the dower rights of widows can be interpreted several ways if seen through today's eyes. Traditionally, a widow received a one-third life estate in her husband's lands. When this right began, all property was real property. Any chattel was attached to the real property. As England modernized, different forms of property appeared: trusts, companies, corporations, and so forth, none of which could be part of the widow's dower. Thus, dower rights almost disappeared in practice because wealthy men would put most of their money into trusts so that they could dispose of it unencumbered. Women had thereby lost a "protection" of the common law. At the same time, they gained more control of their separate property through the establishment of separate estates in equity courts, and by the invention of "pin money" (a legal fiction that a woman owned her earnings) and separate maintenance contracts, which were similar to pre- and post-nuptual agreements. Whether this was a good change or a bad one depends on the interpretation.[30]

Staves stresses that all English law regarding marital property stems from the patriarchal nature of English society. Society was made up of families ruled by the fathers, and the leaders of society saw themselves as fathers to the whole community. This parental role gave them the authority to regulate what went on within the private institution of the family. It was in the public interest to have stable ownership and transference of property, so lawmakers and judges regulated these areas. Staves said that the study of these laws convinced her that there was a cycle regarding marital property. First there would be societal pressure for fairness in the distribution of property, ensuring that widows received something for their contribution to the family. The next stage would be when men, with the help of lawyers, tried to evade those societal pressures. These evasions would reach such proportions as to raise an outcry within society and legislators would intervene with laws designed to protect women and the family. All of the English laws governing marital property served one purpose, according to Staves, and that was the transmission of property from one man to the next, with a woman as intermediary only.[31]

The best work on the interpretation of English common law regarding the rights of women to own and control property in the Colonial and early Republic eras in America is Marylynn Salmon's *Women and the Law of Property in Early America*. She found that while Northern lawmakers tended to believe that husbands would always take care of their wives and that therefore legal protections for married women were not only superfluous but were actually detrimental to family harmony, Southern men took a more jaundiced view. The Southern colonies and states passed laws ostensibly to protect the property rights of married women, because the Southern lawmakers knew that the husband could not be trusted to act always in the best interest of the wife. States such as Maryland, Virginia, and South Carolina passed laws requiring a wife's consent before the husband could convey her property. They also passed laws for the creation of separate estates for the protection of the wife.[32]

Archival sources suggest that even common people relied on the precepts of English law to regulate their conduct. The justices of the peace in Mississippi Territory did their best to protect property rights. Most of the remaining records are from suits for debt, with judgments against defendants and orders to sell their property to pay the debts owed to the plaintiffs. If a single or widowed woman did not make good on her debts, she could be tried in the Justice of the Peace Court. For example, Mary McGill owed John and William Payton twenty dollars, and they sued her for nonpayment. She did not have enough property to sell to pay her debt, so the judge ordered that "for want of such affects then take the body of said Mary McGill and convey her to the jail of said county there to be detained until the debt and costs aforesaid have been paid." The forms used, the sentence, and the result were exactly the same for Mary McGill as they would be for a man in her situation. Single and widowed women could also sue for debt. Mary Morris, among numerous other plaintiffs, sued William Scott for eleven dollars. She won and the court ordered his property sold to pay her debt.[33]

Married women, however, could not sue or be sued on their own because they had no legal identity. Even where the wife was the actual complainant, the husband had to be the one to bring the suit. On January 9, 1804, Charles Coltins and Sarah, his wife, filed assault charges against Jeremiah Jones in Jefferson

County in Mississippi Territory. *Plaintiff* is used in the singular throughout the suit, obviously signifying the husband. The defendant's lawyer tried to get the charges dismissed because the complaint was too vague and did not say where or when exactly the assault on Sarah occurred. This case is treated exactly as it would have been under English law: the wife suffered an assault, but it had to be the husband who brought charges.[34]

The Mississippi Territory did allow married women to be called as witnesses. In the case of *Thomas Calvit v. Philip Alston*, James Truly and Elizabeth Truly were summoned to appear as witnesses. Here the witnesses were treated as two separate people, with *they* being used as the pronoun. Other women, including Frances Odom and Polly Heath, were also summoned as witnesses. No mention was made of their marital status, and each was treated separately.[35]

Wills made and executed during the early national period showed clearly the influence of English common law. The will of William Murray is one example. Though Murray lived in Spanish Louisiana, he had come from Mississippi and wanted his will to follow the laws there. He left his widow, Martha, a life estate in all his property, meaning that none of his land would be sold during her lifetime; then the one-fifth that the law allowed him to dispose of would go to Anna Maria Rumsey, and his son William would be sole other heir. As far as he could accomplish it under Spanish law, Murray made his will conform to English common law, shown by his granting his widow a life estate. He was far more generous than the common law, though, because he left her a life estate in the whole of his property, instead of in merely one-third. Under Spanish law for estates without wills, the widow would have received first her share of the community property, then half of his share of the community, with the remainder going to his heirs and designs. Spanish law also dictated that the testator could not dispose of more than one-fifth of his property to any person outside his immediate family, thus the one-fifth left to Rumsey.[36]

English common law developed as England developed. The laws, court decisions, and procedures all were intended to bring about peace and stability. The protection of property rights was paramount, and English society thought men were more capable of protecting those rights. Property rights, then, were vested in men or were controlled by men, with the intention that married men would use property wisely for the benefit of the whole family. This common law came to the English colonies and spread westward throughout North America with Blackstone's *Commentaries*. The Southern states especially kept with traditional laws governing marital property. When families from these states migrated to Texas, they ran into a legal system based on very similar precepts but far different practices.

★ 8 ★

The Application of Spanish and English Laws to Anglo-American Settlers in Mexican Texas

THE 1820S BROUGHT many changes to Texas. The first of the more important changes was that Mexico, including the region that would become the Lone Star State, gained its independence; the second was that an increasing number of people from the United States immigrated to the area, bringing with them their English common-law background. The resulting clash of culture, societal mores, and legal systems would have a far-reaching impact on what was the province of Tejas. This chapter looks at those changes from the point of view of the new arrivals.

In 1821 Mexico earned its independence from Spain. The new leaders of Mexico planned radical changes in their political institutions. The Constitution of 1824, one of the most liberal in the world, proclaimed among other ideals that all persons should be treated equally. Women's rights, since they were already among the most generous in the world at that time, remained as they had been under Spanish rule. A search of legislative archives of both the Mexican government and the state of

Coahuila y Texas suggests that the legislators in neither federal nor state government made any moves to alter women's rights.[1]

Of far more concern to Mexican authorities were the American immigrants coming into the northern parts of the new nation from the United States. A few Anglo individuals who had little regard for the niceties of legality had already made their way into East Texas. The Mexican leaders knew that they had neither the money nor the manpower to keep the Americans out by force, so they approached the situation in a different manner. One of the first acts of the Mexican government was to confirm in 1821 an empresario grant made to Moses Austin by Antonio María Martínez, the last Spanish governor of Texas.

Moses Austin was born in October 1761 in Durham, Connecticut. He spent his adult years in various business enterprises, never quite gaining the financial success he wanted. As was common in those days, his successive ventures took him farther and farther west. In 1797 he moved to the Spanish territory of Missouri to take up lead mining. There he took the oath of Spanish citizenship and raised his family. The sparse population was still mainly French with only a few Spaniards present. Other Americans were scarce but increasing. Moses's son, Stephen F. Austin, born in Virginia in 1793, grew up in this mixture of nationalities.[2]

The Spanish Crown ceded the Missouri Territory back to the French in 1800; three years later Napoleon sold it to the United States as part of the Louisiana Purchase. The Austins once again lived in American territory. The War of 1812 disrupted the economy of the region, which was depressed even further by the panic of 1819. Moses Austin constantly faced financial stresses, although both he and his son remained highly respected in the community. The territorial legislature nominated Moses Austin to serve as their senator in 1812, but President James Madison did not appoint him. Stephen F. Austin did serve in the territorial House of Representatives from 1814 to 1820, when Missouri joined the Union. This experience would give him a solid background for his later dealings with other governments.[3]

In December 1820 Moses Austin traveled to San Antonio de Béxar to see the governor of Texas and discuss the possibility of setting up a colony in Texas. In a pamphlet written in 1829, Stephen F. Austin told the story of that meeting. Governor Antonio Martínez would not even listen to the senior Austin's proposal and ordered him out of the province immediately. Austin was tired from his journey and in despair, but, while crossing the plaza in front of the Governor's Palace, he ran into an old acquaintance, the Baron de Bastrop. Bastrop intervened with the governor and eventually Martínez approved the application and sent it on to the state capital for final judgment. The commandant general of the Eastern Interior Provinces, Joaquín de Arredondo, approved the petition in January 1821. The fact that Austin had been a Spanish citizen in Missouri apparently was the deciding factor.[4]

Two events occurred later in 1821 that could have spelled the end of Austin's dream of colonization: Mexico won its independence from Spain and Moses Austin died. The Mexican government was under no obligation to ratify deeds by the Spanish government and could easily have rejected the proposal. Had that happened, Stephen F. Austin might have gone in another direction, living an easier but less legendary life. However, Austin chose to carry out his father's dying wish and bring Anglo-American colonists to Texas. In August of 1821,

Austin traveled to San Antonio to request formally that he be made heir to his father's colonization contract. Governor Martínez approved the transfer and Austin's plans for granting lands to the colonists.[5]

Austin acted immediately to influence families to move to his colony. These lands were situated along the middle Texas coast, lying inland to the road from San Antonio to Natchitoches, an area now occupied by twenty-three counties. The first families had already arrived when Austin learned via Martínez that his contract had not yet been approved by the commandant general in Monterrey, who demanded that Austin not begin colonization until the provincial government had examined and approved the plans. Austin would have to travel to Mexico City immediately to preserve the colony.[6]

Texas in the Mexican era. Courtesy of the University of Texas Libraries, University of Texas at Austin.

Spanish and English Laws in Mexican Texas

The details of Austin's journey and his travails with the various Mexican governmental entities are not pertinent to this work. It is necessary only to know that he eventually succeeded in getting approval for his colony. Austin's absence and especially the lack of land laws for the colony caused uncertainty and disturbances there. One of his first actions on his return, in January 1824, was to issue "Instructions and Regulations for the Alcaldes" to quiet the turmoil that had arisen among the colonists during his stay in Mexico City. This included both a civil and a criminal code, and it was an attempt by Austin to apply Mexican laws in a form that Anglo colonists would understand. While in Louisiana, Austin had studied law for a few months and used his knowledge to write the laws for his colony. He apparently reproduced from memory all the forms used in his regulations.[7]

The first article of Austin's Civil Regulations outlined the duties of the *alguacil*, or sheriff. The *alguacil* had to give bond that he would perform his duties faithfully, including handing over any money he collected. The regulation even specified the form that the bond was to follow. The second article gave the form for registering all official acts of the alcalde. An alcalde is usually defined as a mayor or magistrate, but this official had much wider powers than most mayors. He was the chief administrator of the colony and also acted as district judge. He had to record all cases, judgments, and appeals and hand these over to his successor in office. The third article gave the form for filing complaints before the alcalde. The form itself is drawn directly from Anglo-American law, specifically Louisiana law. Mexican law did not mandate the use of such forms: the alcalde was supposed to decide cases on their merit, not on whether the paperwork had been done correctly. This lack of emphasis on forms is a major distinction between Spanish and English legal systems. Austin probably included the forms in these regulations for the precise reason that they were what he and his colonists were familiar with from the United States. Few if any law books existed in Texas, so he incorporated the forms in order that everyone would know what to do.[8]

Articles 4 through 8 covered a defendant's response to summons and what to do if either party failed to appear for judgment. Article 9 reflects the Hispanic influence. If possible, the alcalde was to try to settle the suit amicably. In contrast, Anglo law discourages amicable settlements, as they tend to lower legal fees. Hispanic influence is further demonstrated in article 10. If the case involved an amount over ten dollars, the alcalde would appoint arbitrators to hear the case. However, no jury trials existed under Spanish law, a point that Anglo colonists would find less appealing as time went on. Articles 11 through 14 dealt with qualifications to be an arbitrator, his bonds, and his duties. Articles 15 through 17 covered jurisdiction; eighteen and nineteen dealt with judgments; twenty, the right to appeal and the form to be followed. Articles 21 through 28 described the methods of executing judgments, seizing property, and guarding property against its being removed before judgment could be executed.[9]

In light of the concern of the colonists over their debts incurred in the United States, article 27 is most revealing. It stated that no cause of action accruing outside of Mexico could be pursued in Austin's Colony without permission of the judge of the colony. Considering that Stephen F. Austin was the judge of the colony and he had outstanding debts in the United States that he was struggling to repay, the likelihood of such permission being granted was slim. This lingering concern over debts outstanding in the United States remained a concern with the inhabitants of the Republic of Texas, as revealed in the debates over how and whether to enter the Union. The regulations ended with a list of alcalde, *alguacil,* and constable fees. A final article, added a few months later, detailed how colonists should deal with stray animals.[10]

Austin also wrote criminal codes for the colony. Although this book does not deal directly with criminal law, it is interesting to see how Austin blended Anglo and Hispanic ideals in his criminal codes. The purpose of Anglo criminal laws was to protect property rights, and punishments were intended to deter people from breaking the law. Colonists were accustomed to severe punishments for slight infractions, especially where property was concerned. On the other hand, Hispanic criminal punishments were intended to repair the damage done to the community by the malefactor. Public apologies, fines paid to build churches and municipal buildings, and reparations all served to punish the criminal offender while validating the mores of the community. The criminal regulations, however, rarely needed enforcement. Austin's colonists were noticeably law-abiding, as he and the other leaders expelled troublemakers.[11]

The first five articles of the criminal regulations dealt with the capture and treatment of hostile Indians. Article 6 covered murder, theft, robbery, and all other depredations. It was the duty of all honest citizens to apprehend an evil-doer and bring the criminal to justice. Article 7 outlawed gambling of any sort except horse racing, primarily because racing horses improved the breed. Article 8 proclaimed swearing and drunkenness to be misdemeanors punishable by a fine of up to ten dollars. Men and women living together without benefit of wedding vows had sixty days to get married before they violated the provisions of article 9. Any person, man or woman, convicted of living in sin could be fined up to five hundred dollars and sentenced to hard labor on public works. Articles 10 through 14 dealt with the misdeeds of slaves and the duty of honest citizens to return runaways to their owner. Article 15 covered theft, article 16 covered assault, article 17 dealt with slander, and article 18 outlawed counterfeiting. All such crimes could be punished by fine, redress to the injured party, and hard labor on public works. Articles 19 and 20 told the alcaldes how to handle these cases, and the last six dealt with execution of fines and punishments. Nowhere was there mention of capital punishment, and corporal punishment was limited to slaves, reflecting the Hispanic tradition. José Antonio Saucedo, political chief of the department of Texas, approved both sets of regulations in May 1824, making them the official laws of his colony for the next four years.[12]

One of Austin's next official acts was to distribute the land of his empresario grant to the colonists. Most of Austin's original colonists, called the Old Three Hundred, received their land deeds in the summer of 1824. Austin's original plan for land distribution included giving each man, married or single, 640 acres, adding 320 acres for a wife, 160 for each child, and 80 for each slave. He wanted to sell town lots only to mechanics, merchants, and other professions who needed to be in town for their business. All others would live on their farms. This plan had been approved by Governor Martínez in 1821, but political events in Mexico brought some minor changes to the system of land distribution.

The Sovereign General Congress of the United Mexican States passed the General Law of Colonization in August of 1824. Article 1 "offers to those foreigners who may be desirous

Spanish and English Laws in Mexican Texas 117

of settling in [Mexican] territory security for their persons and property, providing they obey they laws of the country." Taxes would not be collected from colonists for four years after they moved to Mexico, according to article 6, and article 12 limited the amount of property for any person to one square league (five thousand yards) of irrigable land, four square leagues of nonirrigable land, and six more for pasture. Each state was directed to write its own, more specific laws.[13]

In March 1825 the Congress of the state of Coahuila y Texas passed its Law for Promoting Colonization. It was much more detailed than the Mexican national law, being set forth in forty-eight articles instead of sixteen. The state law also limited colonization to those who promised to obey the state and national laws and encouraged settlers to become Mexican citizens as quickly as possible. Article 3 made colonists take an oath to support the Mexican Constitution and "to observe the Religion as stipulated by the former." The amount of land to be given to any colonist was specified as a lot of land five thousand yards on each side, or twenty-five million square yards, which could be subdivided into squares one thousand yards on each side. Each empresario received five lots and five subdivisions of arable land per hundred families brought in, up to a maximum of eight hundred families. Each family received one division of arable land. Cattle raisers could receive an extra twenty-four million square yards of land. The state law recognized the value of having women in frontier areas. Bachelors received only one-fourth the amount of land that a family received, but if that bachelor married a Mexican woman, he could double his landholdings.[14]

Stephen F. Austin followed these regulations when granting land to his colonists, forcing bachelors to join together as "families" and subdivide the land granted to the "family." He also followed the practice of granting land to the head of the household, whether that person was male or female. According to the list of the Old Three Hundred, almost a dozen women received land from Austin in 1824. These women, because they were treated as the heads of families, must have been widows with minor children. Some women are specifically identified in the deeds as widows, as when Elizabeth Kuykendal, *viuda* (widow), sold land to Jonathon C. Peyton in 1831. A woman's marital state made significant differences in her legal capacity under Anglo-American law, so it was important to make note of it in the legal document. Women buying or selling land are identified as widows, spinsters, or married. Married women had to have their husbands join the sale to make it legal. When Louisa Ann Morton, widow, sold land to Henry Austin in 1835, she did so by and with the express consent of her current husband, Daniel Perry.[15]

Once the colonists received their land and began to live on it as Mexican citizens, they soon came into conflict with Mexican laws. These Anglo-American settlers who moved into Texas in the 1820s and 1830s came mostly from the Southern states in the United States. The intention of these immigrants was to expand the realm of "King Cotton" and spread the Southern way of life. People moving from the South did not want to be transformed into Mexicans, for they had little respect for Hispanic culture. In Mexican Texas, they wanted to set up an extension of what they had known while living in the United States. Stephen F. Austin spent much time and energy ensuring that Texans would be allowed to keep their slaves, even after the Mexican government had abolished slavery. The Jacksonian-era immigrants were determined to create an Anglo-American Texas in their own image.[16]

Wherever people go, the institution of marriage follows. In

Austin's Colony, the need for recognizable marriages caused consternation among the settlers. The colonists had grown up with American laws, which derived from English common law. That legal system allowed what were, and still are, called common-law marriages. The English legal system placed a high value on the protection of property rights, and it favored having clear title to property over other legal niceties. Marriages were easy to obtain because property ownership could be more easily decided in a marriage than in a nonmarital partnership arrangement. Marriages were so easy to obtain, in fact, that many people were legally married without even knowing it. All the law required to turn a cohabiting partnership into a marriage was an agreement of both parties to be married, a representation to others that they were married, and physical consummation. Once a couple met all three elements, they were married.

Once married, all the wife's property belonged to the husband, so clear title was established. This desire to stabilize society by affirming title to property was the purpose of common-law marriages in ancient times. A more recent purpose has been to legitimate offspring of nontraditional marriages. The purpose most suitable on the frontier was to allow marriages in the absence of churches and ministers. American pioneers had long relied on common-law marriages as a way to stabilize society when preachers could not be found. Under English and American law, common-law marriages were just as binding, just as legal, and just as legitimate as any marriage celebrated in a church, but not under Spanish law.

In 1821 Mexico gained its independence from Spain, but it retained the Spanish laws and legal system. The Mexican Constitution upheld the Roman Catholic Church as the state religion. The Roman Catholic Church, in the Council of Trent in 1563, had defined a legitimate marriage as one performed by a

Roman Catholic priest in a Roman Catholic church in front of witnesses. The Spanish king, Philip II, issued a proclamation in 1564 that he would implement and defend the orders of the Council of Trent. Philip ordered all clergy in the Spanish empire, which included Texas, though no one but Indians lived there, to publish and obey the orders of the council. Mexico, or New Spain, probably received the word in mid-1565. After that time, the rule of the Council of Trent was the law governing the legitimacy of marriages in Spanish America.[17]

In Mexico, which continued to recognize the Roman Catholic Church as the established church even after independence, only marriages performed by priests in churches were valid. Unfortunately for the inhabitants of Anglo Texas, rarely could they persuade priests to make the trip from civilized, comfortable Mexico to savage, hostile, and dangerous Texas. Also, the Mexican government did not have the funds to provide for priests to make the trip. The lack of priests did not stop people from wanting to get married, and since Austin had outlawed couples' living together without benefit of marriage vows, something had to be done. The result was marriage by bond.

Couples who wanted to get married would make out a bond, just like the bonds that guaranteed debts and good behavior, that guaranteed they would get married by the first priest who came to the area. One hundred marriage bonds were executed in Austin's Colony between 1824 and 1835. The wording of all bonds is almost identical. John Crownover and Nancy Castleman executed the first bond, as follows:

> Be it known by these presents that we John Crownover and Nancy Castleman of lawful age inhabitants of Austin's Colony in the province of Texas wishing to unite ourselves

in the bonds of matrimony each of our parents having given their consent to our union and there being no Catholic priest in the Colony to perform the ceremony—Therefore I the said John Crownover do agree to take the said Nancy Castleman for my legal and lawful wife and as such to cherish support and protect her forsaking all others and keeping myself true and faithful to her alone. And I the said Nancy Castleman do agree to take the said John Crownover as my legal and lawful husband and as such to love honor and obey him forsaking all others and keeping myself true and faithful to him alone. And we do each of us bind and obligate ourselves to the other under the penalty of twenty thousand dollars to have our marriage solemnized by a priest of this Colony or some other priest authorized to do so as soon as opportunity offers. All of which we promise in the name of God and in the presence of Stephen F. Austin Judge and Political Chief of this Colony and the other witnesses hereto signed. Witness our hand the 29th of April 1824.[18]

The marriage bonds executed in Austin's Colony indicate that early settlers tried to comply with Mexican laws. Later colonists also showed that they wanted valid marriages and legitimate children. In the Austin Papers, housed at the Center for American History at the University of Texas, is a letter from Thomas Barnett to Stephen F. Austin. Writing in 1831, Barnett had heard that a priest was soon to visit the colony. He himself was too ill to travel to San Felipe, the seat of government for the colony, and he did not want to leave his family alone for any length of time because of Indian depredations in the area. So he wrote, "I have therefore to request you and through you the Rev[erend] Father Muldoon to call at my house on the way down to the end that the marriage contract betwixt myself and my wife may be consummated and my children christened."[19]

The marriage bond between Thomas Barnett and Nancy Spencer was dated April 20, 1825, so the couple had been living together as man and wife for six years. Their bond, like all others, promised to have their marriage formalized when the next priest came to the area. Father Michael Muldoon was born in Ireland but educated in Spain because British laws forbade teaching the Catholic faith. He was the only priest appointed to serve the Texas area, and then only from 1831 to 1832. Father Muldoon was known for his leniency toward Texas Protestants, so much so that people whose conversion to Roman Catholicism was nominal were known as "Muldoon Catholics." The Barnetts, like most couples who married by bond, wanted to make good on their word and have the priest validate their marriage. No record exists on any couples who, instead of validating their marriages by bond, chose to forfeit them. At least one historian has implied that if both parties reconsidered after filing the bond, all they had to do was get the piece of paper and burn it to be "young as ever and free as the air."[20]

The practice of marriage by bond was so commonplace in Anglo Texas that the Republic of Texas acted quickly to legitimate both marriages and children born to those marriages whose only other validity lay in their bonds. Beginning in 1835, the Consultation acted to legitimate individuals and validate marriages, granting all ministers, judges, and alcaldes the right to administer marriages, and declaring legal "all marriages heretofore celebrated by bond or otherwise." In 1837 the legislature of the Republic passed the Marriage Act, saying that the lack of priests had caused "many persons [to] have resorted to the practice of marrying by bond," and allowed those persons to go before any magistrate to regularize their marriages. Those marriages became legally binding from the beginning, that is, from the posting of the bond, and all children of those marriages were legitimate. Where one spouse had died, the survivor could validate the marriage automatically.[21]

Marriage by bond, then, was a practice that lasted just over a decade, but it explains much about the attitudes of the settlers. Anglo settlers were used to the concept of common-law marriages, but their desire to obey Mexican law would not let them simply declare themselves married. They had to do something that showed an adherence to the Roman Catholic definition of marriage, and that something turned out to be a bond. Bonds were an English invention that guaranteed the good behavior of officials on the threat of their forfeiting the bond money. Bonds also had to be guaranteed by upstanding men in the community who would pay the bond if the official left town suddenly. In this way bonds can be seen as a public display of confidence in a person's behavior.

Given this structure, it makes ultimate sense for marriages to be guaranteed by bond. The whole community suffered when couples could not marry. Men, especially, were thought to be much more civilized once they were married. Both the *Recopilación* and the immigration laws gave preference to married men. It is somewhat ironic, though, that marriage, the most personal of institutions, would be guaranteed by the forfeiture of a bond, one of the most public of institutions. That the Texas settlers employed this innovation, and that they adhered to it, shows they did intend to conform to Mexican law, as long as it was reasonable to do so. When the laws became unreasonable in the minds of the settlers, they rebelled and formed their own republic. Marriage by bond showed an outward acquiescence to Mexican law, while reserving the right for the settlers to make their own accommodations on their own terms.

Similarly, case law in the Nacogdoches Archives shows how Anglo-American immigrants coped with Mexican laws in Texas. These archives contain a mixture of English- and Spanish-language documents from the town of Nacogdoches under Spanish and Mexican rule. The leaders of Austin's Colony all endeavored to learn to read and write Spanish, with varying degrees of success, but many of the colonists did not make such an effort. They still, however, promised to abide by Mexican laws, as witnessed by this letter.

> "Dec 9th, 1829, To the Constitutional Alcalde of the District of Nacogdoches: Sir I received your Communication this morning But as it is in Spanish I do not understand it But as Soon as I can have it translated it Shall be attended to [signed] Yours respectfully, Benjamin Lindsy."

Another bilingual example of Mexican justice concerned a recent widow. On July 31, 1824, Julianna Quirk wrote, in English, to Juan Seguín, who was then Political Chief of the District of Nacogdoches. She requested that he protect her from her late husband's creditors. Her husband had died suddenly and the creditors all wanted to be paid immediately. She had no money at that time but did have a mill and promised to pay off the creditors when the debt came due. Juan Seguín issued an order, in Spanish, for her creditors to stop harassing her.

In the name of the Supreme Executive and in the name of the Mexican Nation, let it be known to any person having any debt against the property of the late William Kirk: Julianna Nores remains obligated to recognize the debts owed by the late Kirk, without any reduction, and will pay them all when they are due. Costs to the said late Kirk. My hand August 8, 1824, Juan Seguín.[22]

Also in 1824, one lawsuit in Nacogdoches followed the Spanish format, with witnesses giving testimony before the alcalde, who rendered judgment. A woman, Caty Hogan, was one of the witnesses and was treated the same as were the male witnesses, again following the Spanish custom. Later lawsuits, however, became more Anglicized. These cases were more likely to follow Anglo patterns than Spanish patterns, especially where the parties to the suit were from the United States. By early 1826, some trials went through the English procedures of grand jury, with lawyers on both sides, and a jury trial, neither of which would be used in Spanish law. Related documents use the terms *venire* (a summons to appear in court) and *true bill* (when a grand jury finds enough evidence to send a criminal case to trial), which are English common-law forms. The listing of cases and outcomes for alcalde's court, entitled "March Term of 1826," gives the names of men who served as jurors, although the documentation is still in Spanish.[23]

In September 1826, Nacogdoches resident Robert Collier died. His wife, Harriet, was named administratrix, as would be normal procedure under either Spanish or English law. Her first act as administratrix was to produce an inventory of the estate, which she filed on September 20. She listed all of their possessions, with a few exceptions, as belonging to him, as they would have done under English common law. These included:

> House, offices, and Negro cabins, 146 acres in cotton, a gin, house, and press; another 60 acres fenced; another plot of 8 acres with unfinished cabin; four Negroes: Matthew, a field hand, 38, Mary, a field hand, 21, William and Daniel both 2, claimed by Mrs. Collier as her own, as gift from her father; Caesar, field hand, 40, Judy his wife, field hand, 38, Caroline, 10, Gill, 8, Rilla, 5, Patsy 3, Gabriel 5 months all children of Judy and Caesar; Dory, field hand, 21, property of Nathaniel Collier [son]; Judy, 21, field hand; Crayton, field hand, 50, his wife Jenny, 60; Joanna, house servant, 14, Sarah, house servant, 25 with her children Eliza, 8, Teno, 5, and Louisa, 1; farming utensils and blacksmith tools; 50–60 head of cattle, 20 head of hogs, 5 mules, 2 jennies, 2 jacks, and a colt, 5 horses and mares and 2 colts; household furniture; mares, jacks, and jennies in possession of Capt. Grosvenor; George, a field hand, 14.

As in the previous case, the husband's creditors wanted to be paid off immediately. Collier petitioned the alcalde for relief from the creditors until she could gather the cotton crop, for then she would be able to pay them.[24]

Apparently Collier was not able to pay off all the debts, because in April 1827, she was sued, in her capacity as administratrix, by James Tate. She was joined in this suit by her new husband, John Roberts. No outcome of this suit remains in the archives, but creditors Harrison and Hopkins won a judgment against John Roberts and wife as curators of the estate of Robert Collier. Here the suit was against the new husband, though the wife/administratrix was named. As under English law, it was the husband, not the wife who was the administratrix, who had to provide bond as defendant. In January of 1828, the same John Roberts and wife filed a plea for justice in the estate of Robert Collier, in response to a suit by yet another creditor, named Bean, who wanted to attach some of the Roberts's slaves in lieu of payment. Harriet testified that the slaves Bean wanted were given to her as a wedding present by her new husband and so were not part of the Collier estate. Here, again, the suit is actually against the wife in her capacity of administratrix; the husband is named as the main party. All the people in these suits follow English law by naming the new husband as the main party, when the widow/wife was the administratrix of the estate.[25]

The administration of the estate of Micajah Munson shows how the American colonists still wanted to follow American laws. Munson died intestate in Nacogdoches in September 1826, leaving a widow, Elizabeth, and two young children. The alcalde named the widow administrator. Women in Mexican Texas did not stay single long: in June 1827 Elizabeth married Samuel Whitney. Whitney now claimed the entire estate as his by virtue of the marriage and proceeded to dispose of it as he pleased. The deceased's brother, Henry, filed suit in September 1828 to stop the wastage of his brother's property. Henry Munson claimed that since the widow had remarried, she should no longer be either administratrix of the estate or guardian of the minor children, as her interests would now be with her new husband. The alcalde agreed and appointed Munson administrator and guardian of the children in September 1828. He filed an inventory a week later that proved to the court that there had indeed been wastage of the estate. Horses had disappeared, cattle had been sold below cost, and the Negroes had been used without compensation to the estate. Elizabeth was found to have been derelict in her duties as administratrix and ordered to pay $572.35 to the estate. All of this followed English law; under Spanish law half of the estate would have belonged to the widow outright as her half of the community property, and half of the remainder would have been hers by intestate succession. The remaining quarter was all that would have gone to the children, and she did not waste their quarter. Under Spanish law, as it should have been applied in Mexican Texas, Elizabeth Munson Whitney would not have been liable.[26]

American women, used to the English legal system, sometimes found it useful to appropriate what little protection it offered them. In legal matters, it was usually easier for a man to go through the court system and get justice, so women appealed to their male protectors. In September 1835, Daniel Wilbourne applied for guardianship of his daughter Milley Berry, widow of John Berry, and her son.

> Honorabel Juge Lues Roguag—Daniel Wilbourne Setler in this Jurisdiction makes it nown to your honour that it is the wish of his Daughter Milley Berry the widow of John Berry Diseast that I should be a Joint guarden for hir and hir son John Berry the son of John Berry Deseast with Antonio Manchak to atend to giting the Property that was left by John Berry Deseast for the Banifit of the air of said Berry and his widow and fulfilling such Deutys as may be to the Benifit of the same Declaring this to be Done in good faith areeable to the wish of Milley Berry widow of John Berry Deseast—Nacogdoches September the 24th—1835

The alcalde granted the request on October 3, 1835. The reason for the petition was that it would be much easier for the widow's father to file all the legal papers and deal firsthand with creditors than it would be for the widow herself. Under Mexican law, she had complete legal capacity, but under American custom, she would have found it difficult to receive justice.[27]

The *ayuntamiento* of San Felipe De Austin, a municipal government similar to *cabildo,* sometimes followed Anglo law and sometimes used Mexican law when deciding suits and petitions of colonists. It cannot be determined why the *ayuntamiento* chose the laws it did, unless they were driven by a sense of justice and used whichever law system brought them closest to equity. On December 6, 1830, the *ayuntamiento* heard a petition from Eliza Grazley for title to certain lots to be granted to her husband, T. J. Grazley. No reason for her husband's nonappearance was given, nor was she expressly mentioned as his agent. The *ayuntamiento* granted the petition and gave title to the husband alone, if he could make improvements on the lots. This followed Anglo law, for under Spanish law the title would be vested equally between husband and wife.[28]

A few days later, on December 15, 1830, the *ayuntamiento* followed Spanish law. Sarah Scily, wife of Green DeWitt, empresario and founder of DeWitt's Colony, petitioned the *ayuntamiento* of Austin's Colony for a league of land. As justification for her petition, she claimed the need to protect herself and her family from her husband's debts. The *ayuntamiento* granted the petition and gave title to the land to the wife. Under Anglo-American law, this action would have made the husband legal owner and manager of the property so that it could be seized by a court and sold to pay his debts. Under Spanish law, it belonged to the wife, so it could not be taken by her husband's creditors. Here, the *ayuntamiento* used Spanish law to protect the wife and family from the husband's debts, a pattern that would be followed many times in later Texas legislation.[29]

The administration of politics was also an amalgamation of Spanish and English systems. On July 7, 1832, the *ayuntamiento* of San Felipe de Austin met in extraordinary session to discuss the restoration of peace at Anahuac. The members present were: "Horatio Chriesman, 1st Alcalde P D McNeil 1st Regidor Wm Robinson 2d Regidor T H Bell 3d Regidor Jesse Grimes 4th Regidor Martin Allen 5th Regidor Henry Cheeves Sindico Procurado." These men were all former Americans using Mexican titles. They all swore "Allegiance to the Federal Constitution of the US of Mexico, the Constitution of Coahuila and Texas, and general Laws of the Nation and State of their adoption," showing their loyalty to Mexico and their desire to abide by the legal system of Mexico.[30]

From 1821 to 1836, people living in Mexican Texas combined various parts of the legal systems that had originated in England and Spain centuries earlier. Though in the early years of colonization Austin's settlers tried to follow the Mexican system, this situation did not last long. In later years new colonists wanted to use the Mexican judicial system as if it were just like the one they had known in the United States, adding only those provisions of Spanish law that would help their cases. Both men and women living in the Anglo colonies presumed that women's rights were the same in Texas as they had been in the United States. Wills, deeds, and court cases all show a continuation of the English common law, with married women having no legal identity and with widows not receiving a community property settlement of intestate estates. Most of the colonists, while promising to follow Mexican laws, actually did little to find out what those laws were. As the years passed and more people migrated from the United States to Austin's Colony, the Mexican laws held less sway over the colonists. Increasingly, the immigrants conformed to the legal system they had known in America, with a few modifications to make it seem as though they were, in fact, following Mexico's laws. Their desire for American-style justice would be a major cause of their movement for independence from Mexico.

★ 9 ★

The Creation of the Republic of Texas and Its Legal System

THE PEOPLE AND EVENTS of the Texas Revolution have long since been adopted into American mythology. Reality, of course, is much more complex than the image. As more Americans migrated into Texas, the community of Texans became more Anglicized, less willing to obey the laws and customs of the Mexican people, whom they deemed inferior. The clashes between the cultures began early in the settlement process and grew steadily worse as the differences in the two legal systems—the one the settlers promised to obey and the one they knew—became more apparent. Anglo settlers began to demand their "natural rights," those rights such as jury trial and representative government that had developed in English common law. Mexican law had no need for such rights because the people were protected by judges and the legal system itself. The conservative Centralist Mexican government viewed such demands as nonsensical, even treasonous, as they reflected the more liberal Federalist point of view.

Spanish and Mexican officials had long feared that United

States citizens would take parts of northern Mexico by force. The activities of early intruders, such as Philip Nolan in the 1790s and Zebulon Pike in 1807, caused great consternation to Spanish officials. Later filibusters such as the team of Bernardo Gutiérrez de Lara and Augustus W. Magee in 1812–1813, and Dr. James Long, with his expeditions in 1819 and 1821, who tried various means to connect Texas to the United States, caused even greater concern. None of the Americans was successful in gaining Texas land for the United States, but these attempts were a major factor in Mexico's decision to allow controlled immigration from the United States in the 1820s. Once Anglo-Americans began to settle Texas, though, some immigrants spurned Mexican laws and tried to reshape Texas in the American mold.[1]

The Mexican government decided that its policy of allowing immigration from the United States was too dangerous, and it passed a law on April 6, 1830, halting all further immigration from that country. Austin, however, used his contacts in the Mexican government to allow existing contracts to be completed. The law also ordered the collection of customs duties in Texas and provided for the garrisoning of troops in the area. Since colonists had been exempt from most taxes and duties before 1830, their imposition coming at the same time as the outlawing of further immigration alarmed the colonists greatly. They did not understand that the use of the military to collect taxes and tariffs was common in Mexico. The United States had no such tradition, and the colonists feared the loss of their "natural" rights and liberty as defined by the U.S. experience.[2]

Juan Davis Bradburn was the military commander at Anahuac, where the customs duties for East Texas would be collected. Bradburn was a native of Virginia, but he had fought for

The Republic of Texas and Its Legal System

Mexico in the war for Mexican Independence and was a colonel in the Mexican army. He was also a Centralist, in favor of a strong central government, as opposed to the Federalists, who wanted more power in the hands of the states. Most Texans naturally favored the Federalist position, so a contest between Centralists and Federalists began in earnest.[3]

Slavery was another issue that persuaded some colonists to consider armed resistance. Mexico had abolished slavery in 1829, though Austin had gained an exemption from this law for Texas. In 1831 Bradburn sheltered some runaway slaves. Their owner hired attorney William Barret Travis to demand the return of the slaves. After legal harassment on both sides, Bradburn used the military to arrest Travis and his co-counsel, Patrick Jack, on grounds of sedition. This action was entirely legal under Mexican law, but Anglo-Americans saw the use of the military in what was to them a civil matter as a sign of tyranny. Soon Bradburn, as the representative of the Mexican institutions, was under siege by one hundred and sixty angry Anglo-American immigrants. When the Texans heard that Antonio López de Santa Anna was leading a Federalist rebellion against Centralist President Anastacio Bustamante in 1832, they wanted to gain his support in order to protect what they saw as their rights.[4]

The colonists' loyalty, however, was not to Santa Anna but to their own perceived interests. Accordingly, when they began to think their rights would not be protected by Santa Anna's government, the *ayuntamiento* of San Felipe de Austin called for a convention to decide how to protect themselves. Austin, who had opposed the convention initially, served as its president and helped set the tone of the convention as mild and lawful. The delegates, who all came from American-settled parts of

Texas, prepared a petition asking for the repeal of the Law of April 6, 1830. They also wanted the admission of Texas as a separate state in the Mexican nation instead of being the lesser part of the state of Coahuila y Tejas.[5]

There was a chain of events over the next six years that led to the establishment of the Republic, but most of these events did not affect the laws of Texas.[6] Of paramount importance to the Texas colonists was Santa Anna's move from Federalist to Centralist ideals. The one-time champion of all liberal causes joined the forces using the rallying cry *"Religión y Fueros"* to show his support of the Church, the army, and other conservative powers. Liberals all over Mexico, including in Texas, were disgruntled and led revolts against him.[7]

Ultimately, the birth of the Republic was assured by the historic battle of San Jacinto on April 21, 1836. Santa Anna himself was a captive of the victorious Texans, who forced him to sign a treaty granting Texas the independence that their government had proclaimed on March 2.[8]

The Texas government, however, had not waited for Santa Anna's capitulation, or even its own Declaration of Independence, to change its legal system. On November 13, 1835, article 6 of the "Plan and Powers of the Provisional Government of Texas" announced that the judges of Texas should decide all cases by laws based on the common law of England with such modifications as circumstances required. The common law was to be the rule of decision in all criminal cases; article 7 guaranteed trial by jury.[9]

Moreover, on January 16, 1836, the Provisional Texas Congress voted that all crimes and misdemeanors should be regulated by the common law of England and that all civil matters, specifically probate and succession, would be governed by the

Civil Code of Louisiana. The Civil Code derived from the Spanish laws, like *Las Siete Partidas,* but had been simplified in that it incorporated the language of the Napoleonic Code. The code did not affect Texans much, as lawmakers paid little attention to it, and this pronouncement was soon superseded by legislative action. The bill also declared all marriages, of whatever form, valid. James W. Robinson, as acting governor, approved the bill on January 22, 1836. Legislators took this action not because they did not like Mexican law, but because they had a much greater familiarity with Anglo-American law.[10]

On March 2, 1836, just after passing the resolution to declare independence, the convention appointed a committee to write a constitution for the Republic of Texas. This constitution, as adopted on March 17, closely followed the constitution of the United States, with only a few changes. A court system modeled on that of the United States was described in article 4, with section 13 declaring, "The Congress shall, as early as practicable, introduce, by statute, the common law of England, with such modifications as our circumstances, in their judgment, may require; and in all criminal cases, the common law shall be the rule of decision."[11]

Most Texans expected that the Republic would, in fact, be short-lived because it would be annexed quickly by the United States, but political considerations kept President Andrew Jackson from pushing for Texas annexation. Jackson did not even recognize the independence of Texas until the last days of his administration. Texas remained a republic from 1836 until 1845.[12]

Politics in the Republic were complicated, based more on personalities than parties. Sam Houston as first president and Mirabeau B. Lamar as his successor were irreconcilable on many matters. The foundering economy, troubling Indian relations, and the struggle for diplomatic recognition were far more pressing issues to most Texans than was establishing a precise legal system. Not until January 1840 did Congress formally enact that the common law of England, where consistent with the constitution or laws of Texas, be the rule of decision in civil matters. This law also repealed all laws passed prior to 1836, except those regarding land grants.[13]

The Act of January 20, 1840, also defined marital property. A wife kept as her separate property all land and slaves owned at the time of her marriage and all personal property that she owned at the time of her marriage or received as a gift or inheritance during the marriage. The increase of separate property slaves would remain separate property. The husband had the power to manage all of the wife's property during the marriage but could not sell it without her consent. The husband also needed to obtain the wife's father's consent before the husband could sell land or slaves belonging to the wife. If the father was dead, the husband had to get court approval. Community property included all property acquired during the marriage and all property brought into the marriage, except the land and slaves, as well as the wife's personal effects. The community property would be liable for all debts of the husband; however, in the case of debts of the wife, it would be liable only for necessities. Courts usually defined necessities as food, shelter, and clothing of the sort the family was accustomed to. Intestate succession followed Spanish law: the surviving spouse received half of the deceased's half of the community property, and the children split the other half equally. The survivor kept the half of the community property that belonged to him or her. If no children existed, all the community property went to the surviving spouse.[14]

The law of January 28, 1840, also gave married women the right to make wills without the consent of their husbands. Under English common law, all the property in the name of the wife belonged to the husband, so she had no right to transfer ownership of it after her death. Under Spanish law a married woman could dispose of her separate property and her half of the community property by her will. The Texas legislature, by enacting a law to this effect in 1840, recognized the inherent inequity in the English common law and preserved some elements of Spanish law. As under Spanish tradition, the husband customarily managed his wife's property, but his powers could be limited by a court. If the husband abandoned his wife or if he wasted the wife's property, the wife could petition the court, and the judge could grant the wife the right to manage her own property. As in the Spanish and Mexican systems, when a husband sold community real property, the wife had to be questioned separately to determine that it was truly her wish to sell the land. For more than a century, all deeds recording sales of community property land included a separate averment by the wife, made to a notary public out of the presence of her husband, stating she agreed to the sale. The need for the wife's consent came directly from Spanish law.[15]

Other laws changed specific parts of common law to match the expectations of Texans. English law had no provision for adoption or legitimation for natural children; Spanish law favored both. The Texas legislature formally granted adoptions and subsequent name changes to three people and officially declared eight others to be the legitimate offspring of their parents. These actions followed Spanish tradition, with the only exception being that it was not the king but the legislature who authorized the changes in status.

Because English law had no form for adoption, the Texas legislators created their own process. This two-part act of law included a name change for the adoptee and the declaration that the adoptee was the legal heir of the adopter. John Finley Collier, son of Harriet Collier who is mentioned in Chapter 8, changed his name to John Finley Roberts when Harriet married John S. Roberts. John Roberts adopted Harriet's son as his legal heir. Similarly, John and Mary Gillespie adopted Mary Nettle, who changed her name to Gillespie and was then their legal heir. George and Mary West adopted Henry Smith as their legal heir, and he adopted their name. The legislature declared the two sons of Stanley C. Robertson by two different women to be his legitimate heirs. Likewise, they declared the son of Allen Vince and Matilda Wellborn to be Vince's legitimate heir. The legislature did not need to declare the child the heir of his mother, because under Spanish law all children, regardless of their legitimacy, inherited from their mothers. Several times the Republic of Texas Congress enacted laws declaring children of a particular marriage to be legitimate. These marriages were probably marriages by bond, as temporary cohabitation did not merit legitimation of resulting children. In 1841 Congress passed legislation legitimating all children whose parents subsequently married, but fathers could still adopt and legitimate natural children without marrying the mother.[16]

Proof that women actually exercised their legal rights can be found in diaries from the Republic of Texas period. Pioneer women did not have time to worry over fine points of law, but when their rights came under question, they did not hesitate to defend them. Adolphus Sterne was a German immigrant lawyer living in Texas during the 1830s and 1840s. His diary is full of dealings with women. He acted as one female client's advisor when she was executrix of her husband's estate. In another case, he needed to get a wife's signature on a deed so it would be valid. He saw to the distribution of an estate equally among sons and daughters. Wives gave him power of attorney to take care of their separate property. All of these actions would have been impossible or illegal under English law, but the laws of the Republic allowed him to follow the Spanish tradition.[17]

The Nacogdoches Archives contain examples of how women used their Spanish-legacy rights to sue and be sued during the Republic era. One enigmatic entry is a revocation of a power of attorney executed by Nancy Walker. She had given her power of attorney to E. O. Lagrand to sue Hiram Walker "for damages in marriage contract." The records do not contain an explanation of this phrase. Apparently Lagrand did not work to Nancy's satisfaction because she revoked the power of attorney so she could sue Hiram in her own behalf. Under English law, she could not have done any of these legal actions. A married woman could not grant power of attorney to sue her husband because she did not have the right herself to sue anyone. She could not bring any legal action because she did not exist as a legal entity. She especially could not sue her husband, because she was legally "covered" by him. Under Spanish law, and under Republic of Texas law, this was not the case.[18]

In 1840 Rebecca Finley sued Vincenta Córdoba for stealing one of her slaves, valued at $1,500. She won the case and was entitled to damages. Her marital status was not mentioned because it was immaterial. By the Act of January 20, 1840, all slaves owned by a wife before her marriage remained her separate property. Finley therefore had to bring suit in her own name whether she was married or not, because the slave in question belonged to her alone. Under English common law, if she was married, her husband would have to bring the suit, and if she was widowed, that would be mentioned in the proceedings to prove she had the right to sue.[19]

Women did not always benefit from this expansion of their legal rights and responsibilities. In November 1840 Sam Houston, the former president of the Republic of Texas, who knew the law as well as any person in Texas, sued Polonia Mineles del Padilla. She was the widow and administratrix of the estate of Juan Antonio Padilla. Houston claimed that the husband had owed him and that the estate was liable. He won the case. The widow had no money to pay the debt, so Houston had the court order that she be evicted from her home. It could then be sold and the proceeds used to repay him.[20]

The Nacogdoches Archives also contain several instances of women buying and selling land. Under English law, married women could not normally own land, so they could not buy or sell it. Widows and spinsters could own, buy, and sell land; their marital status was always mentioned in the transfer to prove they had legal capacity. Under Spanish law, women of any marital status could own land, but land owned by a married woman was usually sold by her husband, with her separate consent, although she could sell it herself if her husband was not present. In the early years of the Republic, land transactions took place with women as buyers and sellers. Their marital status was not always included, nor were separate acknowledgments always performed. In 1837, Sophia Towns, identified by her race, "Colored," but not by her marital status, sold to William Nestles a lot she had bought in 1831. Juliana Sosa was identified as a widow when she sold land to Frost Thorne. When Therés Rodríguez Tobar sold land to Adolphus Sterne, her marital status was not included, perhaps because the land in question had been inherited. All inheritances became separate property so it was hers to dispose of as she wished, even if she was married. Emilia Sophia Forbes bought land from María Josefa Pares, alias "Negrita," and her son José Falcones, and the marital status of neither woman appears on the document. Forbes also bought land from Adolphus Sterne, and again her marital status was not mentioned.[21]

A Supreme Court of the Republic of Texas was authorized by the Constitution of 1836, but it did not meet until 1840. James Collinsworth was elected to the first chief justice position, but he never served, having died in 1838. President Houston appointed John Birdsall to fill the vacancy, but he, too, never called the court into session, probably because not enough justices could be gathered at one time. The Texas Congress elected Thomas Jefferson Rusk to be chief justice in January 1838, but he did not call a session until late spring of 1840. His court heard only a few of the twenty-two cases filed. Of all the Republic and early statehood justices, John Hemphill, who served as chief justice from 1840 to 1842 and from 1846 until 1858, is the most respected, most famous, and most liberal on his interpretations of women's property rights. During the Republic era, however, only one case came to the court to be decided on the facts of domestic relations or marital property law. In *Scott v. Maynard,* the Supreme Court ruled in favor of a wife being able to sell community property in the absence of, or with the consent of, her husband.[22]

Most of the people who immigrated to Texas in the years 1836 to 1845 could be described as Jacksonian Democrats. One defining characteristic of Jacksonians was that they distrusted banks, especially after the Bank War of 1832. They blamed banks for the Panic of 1837, although historians now know this reasoning was incorrect. The Texas immigrants carried their distrust of banks to a higher level. Most of them had left substantial debt behind them in the United States and were not anxious for U.S. creditors to be able to collect on them in Texas. As a result, the question of whether banks should be allowed to operate in Texas became a heated political issue. This issue was resolved when the legislature of the Republic specially forbade the operation of banks in the new nation.[23]

The economy of the Republic was always in trouble. The Lamar administration attempted to stem inflation and provide government funds by printing copious amounts of paper money. The "red-backs" printed during his term depreciated almost immediately to less than ten cents on the U.S. dollar. Texans blamed much of the monetary trouble on banks in the United States and opposed the creation of these nefarious institutions within the Republic. Both Lamar, the second president, and Anson Jones, the fourth and last president, resisted the establishments of private banks in Texas. An act to suppress private banking became law in 1844. This hostility toward banks came from the fear on the part of Texans that banks would seize their hard-won property for debts both ancient and recent. This fear kept many Texans, including Lamar, from desiring annexation in 1845.[24]

During the existence of the Republic of Texas, 1836–1845, all segments of society were unstable. The economy went from bad to worse, political races were bitterly fought, diplomatic recognition came slowly, if at all, and settlers pushed for peaceful coexistence with the Native Americans. The legislature tried to deal with all these problems and more. Texas legislators had little training for their jobs, so the legal system of the Republic grew out of existing Spanish and Mexican law, overlaid with the

English common law, and it was further modified by exigent circumstances. Of all the men in positions of power, the only one who seemed to be concerned about developing a cohesive legal structure was Chief Justice Hemphill, and even he did not accomplish much until after statehood. The problems addressed during this era would also trouble the state of Texas after it finally achieved annexation into the United States of America.

★ 10 ★

The State of Texas and Its Legal System

JAMES K. POLK made the annexation of Texas a prime issue in the 1844 U.S. presidential election. The annexation process was more involved than anyone expected, but Texas finally became a state in 1845. The statehood constitution made several changes from the Republic Constitution, and the state legislature passed several laws dealing with marital property. The state courts interpreted these laws to protect both women and the family homestead, to the detriment of creditors. By 1850 Texas had introduced the concept of community property to the remainder of the United States, some of which adopted the community property system as more equitable to women.

The Republic of Texas had not experienced the successes its founders had envisioned. The economy remained troubled and the government could not pay off its debts. Individuals also could not accumulate enough capital to retire their debts in the United States. The Mexican nation refused to acknowledge the independence of the Republic and invaded the area twice in 1842. Foreign nations hesitated to recognize Texas because they did not want to antagonize Mexico. Thousands of people immigrated from the southern United States, expecting that Texas would soon join the Union, but Whigs and abolitionists blocked this action for years. President John Tyler's Southern leanings prompted Secretary of State John C. Calhoun to negotiate a treaty with the Republic. This treaty would have added Texas, as a territory, to the Union in the Spring of 1844, but it did not receive the necessary two-thirds majority in the Senate.[1]

The annexation of Texas then became the foremost issue in the 1844 presidential election. Henry Clay, as the Whig candidate, tried to avoid taking a direct stand, but most Whigs opposed annexation. The Liberty Party candidate, James Birney, also tried to play down the question, but most party members were against the addition of another slave state to the Union. It was the Democratic candidate, James K. Polk, who campaigned vigorously on the issue of Manifest Destiny, promising to annex both Texas and Oregon. He won the election and proclaimed that the vote in his favor showed that the majority of people in the United States wanted to annex Texas.[2]

President Tyler, motivated perhaps by the desire to steal some of Polk's thunder, began the annexation process in December 1844. He told Congress that the election was a mandate for western progress and that they should therefore annex Texas as quickly as possible, but there were still not enough votes in the Senate to accomplish this by a treaty. Accordingly, Congress passed a joint resolution for annexation. The February 28, 1845, document allowed Texas to enter as a state, not as a territory. Texas would cede to the United States its public edifices such as army and navy bases and fortifications but would keep its public domain in order to pay off its debt. The new state could be divided into as many as five states if the people so chose, and slavery would be allowed in all territory south of the 36° 30' line of the Missouri Compromise.[3]

Tyler signed the resolution, whereupon it went to the Texas government for approval and adoption. Anson Jones, then president of the Republic of Texas, was not as ardently supportive of annexation as were some of his compatriots. Britain and France also opposed annexation, and their ambassadors persuaded Jones to accept a slight delay on the question while they tried to persuade Mexico to recognize the independence of Texas. The people of Texas, however, wanted the annexation process to continue, so Jones called for a convention to meet in July 1845. When the Texas Congress met in May 1845, they approved the convention and adjourned, not even considering the pending offer of Mexico to recognize the Republic.[4]

The only public opposition to annexation came over the issues of banking and creditors' rights. In an open letter to Sam Houston, published in the *Texas National Register,* an author calling himself "an East Texas resident" argued against annexation because Texas was still free of "the villainous banking system." He thought that Texas was a better place to live than the United States because there were "no high tariff men and no nullifiers. We have no abolitionists and no slavery men." He feared that federal laws, when enforced in Texas, would break the unity of the nation, much as it had when enforced in the Southern states.[5]

While the annexation convention was meeting, another article in the same newspaper told of the public's attitude toward banks. The banking system went against society because banks made money without working for it; this, for some, amounted to fraud. This anonymous author feared that if banks were legalized in Texas they would impoverish every citizen. "The system of banking tends to demoralize the community," he wrote. "Banks are dangerous to the state." He also made a strong point when he stated that "[i]f any people in America have been victimized by banking institutions, they are the emigrants of Texas. A large class of the population of this country are Southerners whose fortunes have been ruined by bank speculations."[6]

Members of the convention agreed. Thomas Jefferson Rusk, who presided over the convention, said,

> I consider it a bright page in the history of General Jackson, that he has the honor of giving the blow that will destroy them [banks] upon our continent. And I wish by no vote of mine, here or elsewhere, to authorize the institution of a bank, which may benefit a few individuals, but will carry, here as elsewhere, ruin, want, misery and degradation in its train.

Other members concurred. George William Brown, a delegate from Colorado County said, "I look upon it [banking] as an artifice invented by the cunning, to practice frauds upon the ignorant." The few delegates who favored allowing banks wanted them to be heavily controlled and limited in number.[7]

When the convention met in July 1845, they accepted the invitation to join the United States with only one vote against the measure. The lone naysayer was Richard Bache of Galveston County. His reason for that vote was personal. He had gotten a divorce in the United States before coming to Texas. Apparently he had vowed that he would never again live in the same country as his former wife, so he voted against annexation.[8]

One of the first concerns of the convention was how to keep the property of Texas citizens out of the hands of banks in the

United States. The delegates discussed several proposals to limit the jurisdiction of U.S. courts over property in Texas, at least until the statute of limitations had run out on most people's debts. One proposition was to give to the state of Texas all power to adjudicate the land titles within the state, but a member pointed out that the state constitution could not contradict the U.S. Constitution, so that proposal could not be adopted.[9]

The delegates offered many proposals but could not find a solution to their dilemma until Nicholas Henry Darnell offered the following:

> *Resolved,* that the Committee on General Provisions be instructed to enquire into the expediency of providing by law, at the earliest day practicable, that all or one-half the property belonging to the wife by deed, gift, bequest, or inheritance at the time of her marriage, shall remain the property of the wife, as also one-half of the property of the husband at the time of his marriage shall vest, as also one-half of all the property that shall be acquired after marriage, after payment of all just debts shall likewise vest in the wife; also the proceeds of the property belonging to the wife shall be at her disposal.

Only the last clause was debated and deleted. The rest of the resolution carried. The delegates had found a way to keep family property out of the hands of U.S. banks. Community property could not be seized to pay off the husband's debts. Apparently these delegates wanted, as their primary purpose, to use community property to keep creditors and banks from foreclosing on Texas property, but later judges and lawmakers would use this provision to protect the rights of women in Texas.[10]

The major task of the convention was to write the statehood

constitution. Section 22 of the constitution, dealing with land titles, included a homestead provision. Under this provision, neither the state nor creditors could seize a person's homestead to pay off their debts. The delegates all agreed that the homestead exemption should be included, but they argued over what the homestead should include. The delegates also agreed that a husband should not be able to sell the family homestead without the consent of the wife. Delegate James Davis of Liberty County declared, "The spirit of the age is opposed to taking a woman's bed from under her, if she has a worthless and trifling husband."[11]

The delegates also discussed whether they were protecting only the women and children or all heads of household. The answer was, "We wish only to assert a provision, that if the husband even by his criminal prodigality is reduced to necessity, his wife and little ones may not be turned out of their homes, to satisfy the remorseless cravings of the heartless creditor." All seemed to agree with Thomas J. Rusk, president of the convention, when he said that selling all possession of a debtor's family "is one of the evils attendant upon the credit system, by which thousands have suffered the extremity of penury and want. I believe that the credit system is a great injury to any country, and is productive of very little good." R. E. B. Baylor supported this statement by his experience in Alabama, namely, that a homestead exemption there had been very popular. He was satisfied that this law would protect poor ignorant people, women, and children.[12]

John Hemphill was chairman of the judiciary committee and played an enormous role in defining women's legal rights. The committee, reporting on section 18 of the General Provisions article of the constitution, said that the legislature should define separate and community property and the rules of intestate succession. Hemphill wanted section 18 to read,

> No law shall ever be passed, vesting in the husband, by virtue of marriage, the separate property of the wife, as now recognized by law, or depriving her of the portion of the common property to which she is now entitled, nor shall the separate property of either partner ever be made liable for the debts of the other, contracted before marriage.

The minority report, by John Armstrong and R. E. B. Baylor, showed the influence of English law. They wanted only "one-third part of the property of the husband at the time of his death, including the homestead, to remain to the widow during her widowhood." In effect, they wanted the widow to have the one-third life estate found in English common law.[13]

In a debate the next day on which report to accept, several members voiced their opinions on the subjects of separate property for women and family protection from creditors. Convention president Rusk thought that the common law was not enough protection for women. On the other hand, the laws of Spain took too much power away from the husband. Delegate Gustavus A. Everts wanted to use Spanish laws to protect children but not women, and James Davis wanted to make sure that a wife's separate property included what she brought into marriage and that this property would be protected from the husband's creditors. N. H. Darnell wanted the wife's separate property protections to be part of the constitution, not left to the legislature. He did not trust future legislators to maintain these protections.[14]

Armstrong and Hemphill both argued for their positions. Armstrong said that his position made men and women more equal partners in the community, because he defined a wife's property as all property that she either brought into the marriage or afterward acquired by gift, devise, or descent, while Hemphill's report only protected her land and slaves. Hemphill responded with a history of the law in Texas, showing its derivation from the Spanish legal system, and declared that his stance would protect the wife from "prodigality or fraud" without injuring the rights of the husband. He threatened the convention with the horrible prospect of the common law. That if they did not adopt his position, then:

> all slaves, money and every other species of property, land excepted, which the wife brings with the marriage, or acquires thereafter, become the sole and absolute property of the husband. The whole may be absorbed in the payment of his debts before marriage; may be lost in speculations or at the gambling table; may be wasted and entirely destroyed, or may be given away in the presence of his deserted and beggared wife, to the most unworthy wretches, with the most complete impunity, without responsibility and without impediment interposed or remedy afforded by law.

Despite this prophesy of doom, the convention voted 30 to 19 to adopt the minority position instead of Hemphill's version.[15]

The final version of the separate property definition became section 19 of the statehood constitution. It read,

> All property both real and personal of the wife, owned or claimed by her before marriage, and that acquired afterwards by gift, devise, or descent, shall be her separate property: and laws shall be passed more clearly defining the

rights of the wife, in relation as well to her separate property, as that held in common with her husband. Laws shall also be passed providing for the registration of the wife's separate property.

The next section reserved all property rights as they had been during the Republic. This section preserved authentic land titles for all people in general, but specifically ensured that a woman's separate property during the Republic era would remain her separate property after statehood:

> The rights of property and of action which have been acquired under the Constitution and laws of the Republic of Texas shall not be divested; nor shall any rights or actions, which have been divested, barred, or declared null and void, by the Constitution and laws of the Republic of Texas, be re-invested, revived or reinstated by this Constitution; but the same shall remain precisely in the situation which they were before the adoption of this Constitution.[16]

The homestead clause, article 7, section 22, was designed to protect all of the family from foreclosure by creditors. The section also kept the Spanish-heritage rule that the husband had to have the wife's consent to sell the homestead. Section 22 read:

> The Legislature shall have power to protect by law from forced sale a certain portion of the property of all heads of families. The homestead of a family not to exceed two hundred acres of land (not including in a town or city) or any town or city lot or lots in value not to exceed two thousand

dollars, shall not be subject to forced sale, for any debts hereafter contracted, nor shall the owner if a married man, be at liberty to alienate the same, unless by the consent of the wife, in such manner as the Legislature may hereafter point out.

These three clauses demonstrate the desire of the convention to protect family property from creditors, while leaving most of the details to the legislature. Texas voters overwhelmingly approved the constitution in October 1845. President Jones signed it into law on December 29, 1845. In a ceremony at the new state's capitol on February 19, 1846, Jones proclaimed, "The final act in this great drama is now performed; the Republic of Texas is no more."[17]

The legislature quickly took up its duties; the first session of the Texas state legislature met from February 16 to May 13, 1846. Most of the laws passed during those three months were to organize the state and delineate the duties of various officials. By far the most numerous type of legislation was that which set up the new counties. The second most numerous type of law defined the boundaries of the new counties. Some atypical laws were those that established the Odd Fellows and Free Masons in Texas, and one that prohibited individuals from printing promissory notes. The first major law established the militia: it passed on April 21, 1846. A week later the first tax law in the state passed, on April 28, and the next day the legislature continued its work begun in the constitutional conventions by defining women's separate property in a way that protected it from creditors of the husband.[18]

The law of April 29, 1846, "An Act to Provide for the Registration of the Separate Property of Married Women," identified a wife's separate property as, "all property, real and personal, owned or claimed by married women, or which may be owned or claimed at the time of the marriage, by any woman, or which they may acquire by gift, devise, or descent." To be protected from her husband's creditors, the property had to be registered in the county where it was actually located, and, if the wife lived elsewhere, it also had to be registered where she lived. Once her separate property was so registered, it could not be used to pay her husband's debts.[19]

The next day, legislators passed a related law. The law of April 30, 1846, "An Act Defining the Mode of Conveying Property in which the Wife Has an Interest," set forth the form of the privy examination. The wife had to be taken apart from her husband and declare to an uninterested party, usually a notary public, that she was making the sale of her own free will, that she realized what she was doing, and that her husband had not pressured her in making the sale. The law specifically included "land, slave or slaves, or other effects, or the homestead of the family," in which the wife might have a proprietary interest. Section 3 declared that the law applied to the family's homestead as defined in the constitution and to "property owned or claimed by the wife before marriage, and that acquired afterward by gift, devise, or descent." Section 4 repealed all previous laws regarding the wife's sale of property. The legislators intended this provision to protect women from unscrupulous husbands, preventing the husband from selling the wife's property without her knowledge or consent, as he was entitled to do under English common law. The Spanish concept of the wife's partnership in the marriage was used here, as it was in Spain, for the protection of the wife from her husband, not from her husband's creditors. In Texas, both during the Republic and after statehood, these precepts that had originated under Spanish law were applied to keep creditors from taking the husband's property.[20]

The state legislature also passed a private law—that is, a law administered between citizens as opposed to one enforced by the state—that shows it wanted to promote stable marriages and family life in Texas. On April 4, 1846, the legislature legalized the marriage of Samuel M. Parry and Elizabeth Neese. This putative marriage had apparently been in existence for some time, because the law also legitimated the eight children of that marriage. These three laws were the only ones passed by the first legislature regarding the rights of women. The final weeks of the session were filled by the processes of setting up the new government.[21]

The constitution declared that the state legislature should meet only every other year. In 1848, the new legislature met and passed a few laws that affected the rights of women. These laws were part of the intestate succession process delineated in the law of March 18, 1848. This law mingled the English and Spanish procedures, giving equal rights of inheritance to heirs of both genders. Section 3 of that law stated that it did not matter whether the intestate estate came from the father or the mother, from separate or community property, or through purchase by the intestate. All property rights were acquired in the same manner regardless of where the property came from.[22]

Section 4 declared that the property of an intestate survived by a spouse should be divided as follows: If the deceased had children, the surviving spouse received one-third of the personal estate, not including slaves, with the other two-thirds going to the children. The surviving spouse also received a life estate in one-third of the land and slaves of the deceased, with the remainder going to the children. If the deceased had no living descendants, then the surviving spouse received all of the personal estate, except slaves, and a life estate in one-half of the land and slaves, with the remainder going to the deceased's parents and siblings as prescribed in other parts of the law. If the deceased had no living relatives, then the surviving spouse received all of the personal estate. Note that all of the above applied only to the separate property and the one-half of the community that was owned by the deceased. The surviving spouse received his or her half of the community before the rest of the property was distributed.[23]

On March 20, 1848, the legislature passed another law dealing with the probate of estates. Section 24 stated that when a married woman acted as executrix or administratrix, she had to have her husband join with her to get her bond. That bond would then bind her as if she were a femme sole, that is, she could not repudiate it on the grounds that she, as a married woman, lacked capacity to make a binding contract. The husband and wife acted jointly in her capacity as executrix or administratrix. The husband would be liable for the acts of the wife, even when she was representing an estate.[24]

An interesting law showing that the legislature assumed that a married woman was incapable of acting on her own behalf passed on March 1, 1848. This act authorized Sarah Ann Kelton, wife of Oliver P. Kelton, to sell her own property. Oliver had been confirmed a "lunatic" and therefore was unable to manage the community business, so the law said that "she is hereby authorized to sell and convey her separate property, consisting of real estate and Negroes, and otherwise to transact business as a femme sole." All her acts concerning the management of her property were declared valid, "laws to the contrary notwithstanding." This special circumstance shows that the legislators of Texas, representing their constituents, believed that married women should not be conducting business, even when it pertained to their separate property. It took the declaration of incompetence of the husband to allow the wife to sell her own property. The law did not allow her to sell any part of the community or to manage the separate property of her husband.[25]

The third regular meeting of the legislature of the state of Texas took place in 1850. The only law passed that concerned the family was "An Act to Prescribe the Mode of Adoption." During statehood, the legislature had passed various laws authorizing name changes for adoptees and declaring them to be the legal heirs of their adoptive parents, but in 1850 the responsibility for adoption shifted to the county clerks. From that time forward, all adoption would be registered by the county clerk in the county of residence of the parties. Adopted parties were to be treated the same as biological children, except that adopted heirs could not inherit more than one-fourth of the adopter's estate that could be distributed by will. After the passage of this act, the legislature did not authorize any additional adoptions.[26]

The Texas Supreme Court also had a chance to speak on the issue of women's rights during the first few years of statehood. Chief Justice John Hemphill wrote most of these opinions and usually drew heavily upon Spanish law in making his decisions. The other justices seemed just as concerned about protecting women but drew their arguments from English equity courts and the common law as practiced in the Southern states. The first such case was *H. C. McIntire v. Harriet C. Chappell*. Chappell, a married woman, sued McIntire. The defendant pleaded that, because she was a married woman, her husband had to join the suit for it to be valid. Her husband refused to join her in her lawsuit, so the question to the Supreme Court was, was it absolutely necessary to have the joinder of the husband? In his decision, Hemphill reviewed the laws of England and Spain, both of which preferred the husband to bring suit in his own name or that the suit be in the name of both, jointly. Here, however, the husband had refused to join. Hemphill ruled that the husband's refusal could not take away the wife's right to sue. His joinder was supposed to protect the wife, not to deny her any rights. Hemphill declared that the wife had the right to sue in this case.[27]

A similar case came to the court in 1849. *Mitchell & Mitchell v. Wright, Administratrix* began as a probate matter that included a divorce. Mrs. Wright was the administratrix of the estate of Peter N. Hays. Mitchell & Mitchell owed her money in her capacity as administratrix, but when she tried to sue to collect the note, they claimed that she lacked capacity as a married woman. John D. Wright, her husband, refused to join her in this suit, because they were getting a divorce at that time. The law of 1848, section 24, required the joinder of the husband when a married woman acted as administratrix. Justice Abner S. Lipscomb's opinion followed the law, that a married administratrix must be joined by her husband and that she could not act alone to collect the note due her as an administratrix. The case was remanded, to allow her to introduce evidence that her husband had refused to sign. Even though a divorce was pending, she was still a married woman and still had to abide by the laws regulating that group. Also, many divorce cases filed at that time were never finalized, so it could not be assumed that the marriage was ended.[28]

In 1849 the Supreme Court heard the case *Callahan v. Patterson and Patterson.* The Pattersons had sold land to Callahan to pay the debts of Sarah E. Patterson, contracted before her marriage to James D. Patterson. Sarah, being ill, did not make the fifteen-mile trip that would have been necessary to make a privy examination as part of the sale. Sarah then died, and her heir, Robert Patterson, sued to void the sale of the property. Abner Lipscomb wrote the majority opinion in this case. Apparently forgetting that he was the author of section 19 of the General Provisions title of the Texas constitution, Lipscomb wrote, "It seems to have been a favorite object of the framers of our Constitution to secure to the wife her separate property." He then quoted the definitions of a wife's separate property and the act defining the mode of conveyance of that property. That law required the privy examination of the wife before the sale of any property in which she had or may have had an interest. Because Sarah was not privily examined, the deed could not take effect.[29]

Lipscomb went on to examine whether the plaintiff had any remedy in equity. He ruled that the separate property of a wife was liable for debts contracted by her before marriage; that the husband had a duty to support his wife and their children; that he should first do this out of the community property, but if necessary out of his own separate property; and that if the husband could not support the family, then the property of the wife was liable for that purpose. The case was affirmed without prejudice, leaving the creditor able to sue again if he could prove that his debt should be paid from Sarah's separate property.[30]

Hemphill dissented from this opinion. He questioned whether the law as it read allowed a wife to make a full conveyance in cases where that might defraud the husband of his rights. Here, the wife indicated that she intended to convey her separate property to pay her own debts, and Hemphill thought she should be able to do so. He wanted femme coverts (married women under the control of their husbands—the normal condition) to be able to sell their separate property as if they were femme soles (married women either judicially separated from or divorced from their husbands and so not under their control), but the law did not quite allow this. Hemphill said the law went against the doctrine of fairness in law.[31]

In the same session, the court heard the case of *McIntyre v. Chappell*, [sic] now returned to the Supreme Court on other points of error. Here, the full facts of the case are given. James McIntyre married Harriet in Tennessee in 1840, with the intent of moving to Texas. James went to Texas alone, planted crops, and improved the land before returning to Tennessee to bring his wife back to Texas. At the time of the marriage, each party owned slaves in Tennessee. James sold some of these slaves in Tennessee and brought others to Texas. He died in 1844. His widow, Harriet, married the defendant Chappell, who sued to recover some of the slaves on behalf of Sarah McIntyre, minor heir of James. The suit turned on which law ruled the sale of the slaves in Texas, the common law as it was followed in Tennessee or community property law as practiced in Texas.[32]

Justice Wheeler wrote the decision. He said that Tennessee was the domicile of the couple when they married, so Tennessee law applied. Under that law, as in the common law, all of a wife's property became the husband's property upon their marriage, so full title to the slaves vested in the husband. He could sell them freely without her knowledge or consent. Also, in Texas in 1840, the common law as practiced in Louisiana was the law of the land, so again, the slaves of the wife belonged to the husband. Even in Texas, property was presumed to be community property unless proven to be separate, so again, the husband had the right, in 1840, to sell the property. However, the child born to the slaves after the move to Texas was an increase of either separate or community property, and therefore belonged to the community. Community property must go to the heirs of the deceased, in this case, to the minor Sarah McIntyre.[33]

Chief Justice Hemphill's decision in *Cartwright v. Hollis and Wife* gives a good overview of the common law and Texas law concerning the wife's ability to dispose of her separate estate. In 1846 William Hollis tried to buy supplies for his plantation from a man named Cartwright. Hollis had no money and no separate property of his own, nor was there enough community property held by the couple to use as collateral for the supplies. Elizabeth Hollis, however, had a large amount of separate property, including land, cattle, and slaves. Apparently the plantation belonged to her, although that was not entered into evidence. She and her husband executed a joint promissory note to pay for the goods, and Cartwright agreed to this deal. When Cartwright tried to collect the note, the Hollises refused to pay it, saying that the separate property of the wife could not be used as collateral for the husband's debts.[34]

The question of the case was whether a married woman could contract away her separate property by means of a joint promissory note. Hemphill discussed the common law, namely, that the husband had complete management of the wife's property. Under that system, the wife could not make a promissory note, a form of contract, even with her husband, because she had no legal existence separate from him. Equity courts, however, did allow that the wife had her own existence and could control her separate property in limited circumstances. Hemphill then discussed the Texas law of 1840, which declared that the separate property of the wife remained hers throughout the marriage but that the husband had sole management of it. The fourth section of that law made the wife's separate property liable for her necessaries. Hemphill pointed out that it was difficult to tell from the 1840 law what part of the wife's separate property was and was not liable, and exactly what constituted necessaries.[35]

Hemphill declared that the law of 1840 did not intend to allow the husband to encumber the wife's separate property for his own gain, but merely to allow him to run the daily business of raising crops, for example, without having to get a notary to validate each act of plowing, planting, and reaping the wife's separate property farm. The wife's separate property was protected by the statehood constitution. Hemphill's decision stated,

> Such laws as have for their object the preservation of the estate and the wife's rights from the influence of her affection for her husband, or from his fraud, oppression, and circumvention, or that of others, should be enforced according to their spirit and intention, but not so construed as to deprive the wife, or the husband as her legal agent, of the power of contracting for the supplies necessary for the use of such property.

When a wife voluntarily consented to the alienation of her property for the benefit of the rest of her property, she could be held to her contract.[36]

William and Elizabeth Hollis had another case before the Supreme Court that year. In *Hollis and Wife v. Francois and Border*, Chief Justice Hemphill again had the opportunity to expound on the issue of a wife's separate property. In November 1845, the Hollises executed a mortgage on two of Elizabeth's slaves to buy farming implements. The mortgage included a privy examination of Elizabeth that followed the forms prescribed by law for a married woman to dispose of her property. When Francois and Border tried to collect on the mortgage, the Hollises refused to pay, saying that Elizabeth, as a married woman, could not be held to a contract.[37]

Hemphill agreed that under common law, Elizabeth would not be liable for the contract. However, this mortgage was not made in a common-law state, but in Texas, where statutes controlled a wife's power to alienate her separate property. Here, there was no fraud or coercion on the part of the husband, nor was their fraud on the part of the creditor. The general rule was that when a husband and wife jointly encumbered his, her, or their property, the debt was to be paid first out of the community, then out of his separate property, and lastly from the wife's separate property. William Hollis had no separate property and there was no community property, so Elizabeth Hollis's separate property became liable for the debt. This rule was especially applicable when the debt incurred accrued to the benefit of the wife's separate property, as was the case here. The farming utensils purchased with the mortgage were used on her separate property farm. The wife can, therefore, under Texas law, validly encumber her estate, if she waives her disabilities by privy examination.[38]

The case of *Edrington v. Mayfield and Wife* also involved a wife's separate property. The Mayfields lived in Texas, but they went to visit relatives in Tennessee. During this visit, the wife's uncle gave the wife a slave. In 1845, after the couple and the slave returned to Texas, the slave was levied upon to pay the debts of the husband. Hemphill ruled that the laws of Texas, not those of Tennessee, controlled the gift of the slave. Although under Tennessee's common law the slave would have been liable for the husband's debts, that was not the rule in Texas. Under Texas law, gifts remained separate property, so the slave, though given in Tennessee, was the wife's separate property and could not be seized to pay the husband's debts. The opinion stated, "The capacity of the wife to hold property in her own right, separate and apart from her husband, is as complete and perfect as the right of the husband to hold property in his own right separate and apart from the wife. *There is not the slightest difference in this particular between their civil rights and capacities.*"[39]

Justice Lipscomb wrote the last decision of the 1850 session of the Supreme Court that dealt with a wife's separate property. *Blanchet v. Dugat and Another* concerned the wife's ability to manage her separate property. The facts of the case were that the sons of the wife, from a previous marriage, removed her separate property from premises belonging to the husband. The wife consented, even instigated, the removal of her property, but the husband did not consent. The husband sued to recover the property, claiming that he had entire control of it during the marriage and that when the sons came onto his premises without his knowledge or consent, they were guilty of trespass. Lipscomb took up the question of trespass first. He ruled that the wife often had to act as the husband's agent during his absence, even in the management of his separate property. If a wife called in neighbors to help control a husband's unruly slaves during his absence, that would not be a trespass. Even more strongly then, when a wife was controlling her own property, the persons who entered the husband's premises would not be guilty of trespass.[40]

The husband's absence implied an agency in the wife. The sons had no reason to believe that the husband had not consented to the removal, or at least there was no such evidence presented at the trial, so they could not be guilty of trespass. Lipscomb also ruled that the wife has the power to control her separate property in the husband's absence. He wrote, "If, under certain circumstances, she could exercise a control over the husband's property, most assuredly she could exercise such power over her own separate property in his absence." Lipscomb here was protecting the property rights of the wife even over the objections of the husband during the marriage.[41]

In the early years of the state of Texas, legislators and judges worked to protect the property rights of married women. Some men, like the convention delegates, saw women's separate property as a way to protect the family from creditors, while others seemed to view women's protection as a good thing in itself—very much a Southern gentleman's approach. At the constitutional convention, the separate property issue was definitely seen as a way to keep family property out of the hands of creditors. The concept of equity also played a part in these men's actions as they used homestead laws to prevent seizure of the family home by creditors. Because these men's motivations can be interpreted only through their actions, it is impossible to say which idea, fairness or fear of foreclosure, influenced which man more. There is also the factor that providing women with property rights would keep them from becoming a burden on society. The same men who wrote the constitution later served as legislators and judges, and in those capacities they continued to expand and enforce the rights of women to keep and control their separate property. Just as during the Reconquest, in a frontier situation where women were necessary to survival, their rights were protected.

Having these rights did not always lead to happiness. In

some cases, the right of women to control their property worked to their disadvantage, as their property could be seized to pay their debts. Overall, though, because of the actions of these Texas men, Texas women found themselves on a far more equal footing regarding property rights than anywhere else in the United States.

Conclusion

THE MARITAL PROPERTY laws that developed in Texas by 1850 remained in force until the 1960s. During that century, marital property laws were enforced mostly in divorce cases and in the settlement of estates. The laws themselves were not questioned as lawyers used them to win cases for their clients. The idea of community and separate property was finally clarified and codified in the laws of the *Texas Family Code* of 1964. There, Subtitle B covers property rights and liabilities, with Chapter 3 specifically covering marital property rights. In Subchapter A, separate property is defined as "(1) the property owned or claimed by the spouse before marriage; (2) the property acquired by the spouse during marriage by gift, devise, or descent; and (3) the recovery for personal injuries sustained by the spouse during marriage, except any recovery for loss of earning capacity during marriage." Community property is defined simply as "the property, other than separate property, acquired by either spouse during marriage."[1]

In 2005, nine states used community property laws. They

are Arizona, California, Idaho, Louisiana, Nevada, New Mexico, Texas, Washington, and Wisconsin. These marital property laws become most significant in cases of divorce or intestate succession, but they also matter considerably when a couple is buying or selling property and filing income taxes. Also, the whole idea of marriage as a joint venture, instead of one person being in total control, has become more widespread.

Thus, the idea of a ganancial marriage that was prevalent in the Iberian Peninsula after the fall of the Roman Empire has become accepted in the United States. As these ideas became customary law in Castile through the process of Reconquest, as respectable women were lured to settle on the frontiers of Christian Spain, they also found acceptance on the frontier of Texas, where they were just as suitable. Anglo-American men recognized that women contributed significantly to the settlement of the frontier, and they were willing to grant those brave pioneer women substantial property rights in return for their efforts. Some of those men also realized that separate property could be a way to keep family lands out of the hands of creditors pursuing payment for a husband's debts.

During the nineteenth and twentieth centuries, other states recognized the usefulness and practicality of the community property system and adopted it for themselves. It was, after all, far easier to implement than equity courts. Few lawyers, and even fewer nonlawyers, though, realize that these ideas came from Spain, arriving in the United States by way of Spanish conquest of the New World, via Texas. Other Spanish customs, such as adoption and homestead exemption, while not the focus of this work, also became acceptable in the United States.

Her property, his property, and their property—the concept of equality in a marriage that exists within the community property system—seems very American. It is a very democratic notion that all people, even married women, should be able to control their own assets. It is a very republican notion that all people should profit from their exertions and that they should be free to own the results of their labor, even if they are married women. Equality, fairness, and freedom are the ideals that Americans hold dear, even if they are exemplified by laws that originated in Spain.

Appendix A

Chronology

209 B.C.E.	Beginning of Roman conquest of the Iberian Peninsula
27 B.C.E.	Iberian Peninsula pacified and occupied by Rome
98 C.E.	Trajan, first Roman emperor of Spanish origin, begins his rule
264	Franks and Suevi invade peninsula
411	Barbarians sign alliance with Rome, establishing military colonies
568–586	Visigothic King Leovigild expels Roman bureaucracy and unifies peninsula
587	Leovigild's heir, Recared, converts to Catholicism
633	Fourth Synod of Toledo declares it has the power to confirm elected kings
711	Muslim troops under al-Tariq cross the Strait of Gibraltar and defeat King Rodrigo at a battle in Guadalete
718	Pelayo, an elected Visigothic king, defeats the Muslim army at Alcama, beginning the Reconquest
750	Christians under Alfonso I occupy Galicia
778	Defeat of Charlemagne at Roncesvalles, death of Roland

APPENDIX A

791–842	Alfonso II prevails and settles lands south of the Duero River
873–898	Wilfredo the Hairy establishes a Christian kingdom independent of Franks
930–950	Ramiro II, king of León, defeats Abd al-Rahman III
981	Ramiro III is defeated by Almansur, must pay tribute to Caliph of Córdoba
999–1018	Alfonso V of León restructures his kingdom
1000–1033	Sancho III of Navarre subdues Aragon, takes possession of Castile, and proclaims himself emperor, but empire is divided upon his death among his three sons: Navarre to Garcia III, Castile to Fernando I, Aragon to Ramiro I
1035–1063	Fernando I of Castile forces Muslims in Toledo, Seville, and Badajoz to pay tribute. On his death, kingdom is divided between his sons: Castile to Sancho II and León to Alfonso VI
1065–1109	Alfonso VI reunites Castile and León, takes Toledo
1086	Muslims of Granada, Seville, and Badajoz call in Almoravids as allies against Christians
1102	African Muslims occupy Iberian Peninsula to Zaragoza
1118	Alfonso I of Aragon conquers Zaragoza
1135	Alfonso VII of León proclaimed emperor
1151	Almohades replace Almoravids and retake Almaría
1162	Alfonso II unites Aragon and Barcelona
1195	Almohades defeat Castilians at Alarcos
1212	Alfonso VIII of Castile, with help from Sancho VIII of Navarre and Pedro II of Aragon, wins at Las Navas de Tolosa
1229	Jaime I of Aragon reconquers Mallorca
1230	Alfonso IX of León takes Mérida and Badajoz
1217–1252	Fernando III, king of Castile and León, conquers all of Muslim Spain except Granada

Chronology

1252–1284	Alfonso X, the Wise, faces the Mudéjar revolts of Andalusia and Murcia, drafts the *Fuero de las leyes* and later *Las Siete Partidas*
1284	Dissident nobles depose Alfonso X; his son Sancho IV takes power
1309	Fernando IV takes Gibraltar
1312–1350	Alfonso XI fights Granada for twenty-five years, wins battle of Río Salado in 1340
1369	Pedro the Cruel of Castile is murdered by his half-brother Henry of Trastámara, who then rules as Henry II
1464	Henry IV of Castile disinherits his daughter Juana "la Beltraneja" and names his half-sister Isabella as his heir
1469	Isabella of Castile and Fernando, prince of Aragon and king of Sicily, wed
1474	Civil war in Castile between supporters of Isabella and Juana "la Beltraneja" ends in victory for Isabella
1479–1516	Reign of Ferdinand and Isabella (to 1504) and Juana (to 1516)
1492	Ferdinand and Isabella complete Reconquest by defeating Granada; discovery of New World
1503	Creation of the *Casa de Contratación*
1504	Isabella dies, Castile is ruled jointly by Ferdinand and their daughter Juana, though Juana was declared insane most of the time and Ferdinand ruled in her name
1516	Ferdinand dies, crown goes to Charles I of Spain, later (1519) Charles V of the Holy Roman Empire
1524	Creation of the *Real Consejo de Indias*
1556	Charles I abdicates; Philip II takes power until 1598
1558	Defeat of the Spanish Armada by English navy and bad weather
1598–1621	Reign of Philip III
1621–1665	Reign of Philip IV

APPENDIX A

1665–1700	Reign of Charles II
1700	Hapsburg dynasty in Spain ends with death of Charles II; War of Spanish Succession begins
1700–1746	Reign of Philip V
1746–1759	Reign of Ferdinand IV
1759–1788	Reign of Charles III
1763	Treaty of Paris gives all land west of Mississippi River to Spain
1776	Creation of the Commandancy General of the Interior Provinces
1788–1808	Reign of Charles IV
1800	Spain cedes Louisiana to France
1803	Louisiana Purchase
1808–1814	Joseph Bonaparte on throne of Spain
1810	Miguel Hidalgo begins struggle for Mexican independence
1819–1821	Adams-Onís Treaty certifies Texas as belonging to Spain
1821	Mexico gains independence from Spain; Moses Austin receives empresario grant to settle Texas
1836	Texans declare independence from Mexico, set up Republic of Texas
1845	Texas joins the United States

Appendix B

Texas Constitution of 1845

We, the people of the Republic of Texas, acknowledging with gratitude the grace and beneficence of God, in permitting us to make [a] choice of our form of government, do in accordance with the provisions of the Joint Resolution for annexing Texas to the United States, approved March 1st, one thousand eight hundred and forty-five, ordain and establish this Constitution.

. . .

ARTICLE 7. General Provisions.

. . .

SECTION 19. All property both real and personal of the wife, owned or claimed by her before marriage, and that acquired afterwards by gift, devise, or descent, shall be her separate property: and laws shall be passed more clearly defining the rights of the wife, in relation as well to her separate property, as that held in common with her husband. Laws shall also be passed providing for the registration of the wife's separate property.

. . .

SECTION 22. The Legislature shall have power to protect by law from forced sale a certain portion of the property of all heads of families. The homestead of a family not to exceed two hundred acres of land (not including in a town or city) or any town or city lot or lots in value not to exceed two thousand dollars, shall not be subject to forced sale, for any debts hereafter contracted, nor shall the owner if a married man, be at liberty to alienate the same, unless by the consent of the wife, in such manner as the Legislature may hereafter point out.

Notes

Introduction

1. David J. Weber, *The Spanish Frontier in North America* (New Haven: Yale University Press, 1992), 336.

Chapter 1

1. *The Visigothic Code (Forum Judicum)*. Translated and edited by S. P. Scott (Littleton, CO: Fred B. Rothman & Co., 1982), 120–123; Derek W. Lomax, *The Reconquest of Spain* (London: Longman, 1978), 10–24.
2. Joseph F. O'Callaghan, *A History of Medieval Spain* (Ithaca, NY: Cornell University Press, 1975), 52–53; Lomax, *Reconquest*, 21–24.
3. O'Callaghan, *History*, 93–101; Lomax, *Reconquest*, 25–34. See also Roger Collins, *The Arab Conquest of Spain: 710–797* (New York: Basil Blackwell, 1989).
4. O'Callaghan, *History*, 100–115; Lomax, *Reconquest*, 35–40.
5. O'Callaghan, *History*, 116–190; Lomax, *Reconquest*, 41–67; Roger Collins, *Early Medieval Spain: Unity in Diversity, 400–1000* (New York: St. Martin's Press, 1983), 183–224.
6. O'Callaghan, *History*, 193–330; Lomax, *Reconquest*, 68–128; Collins, *Early Medieval Spain*, 225–253.

7. O'Callaghan, *History,* 333–427; Lomax, *Reconquest,* 129–166; Collins, *Early Medieval Spain,* 225–253.
8. O'Callaghan, *History,* 435–445. See also J. N. Hillgarth, *Precarious Balance, 1250–1410,* vol. 1 of *The Spanish Kingdoms, 1250–1516,* 2 vols. (Oxford: Clarendon Press, 1976).
9. O'Callaghan, *History,* 445–449; Lomax, *Reconquest,* 161–166.
10. Peggy Liss, *Isabel the Queen: Life and Times* (New York: Oxford University Press, 1992), 75–78; Stanley G. Payne, *A History of Spain and Portugal,* 2 vols. (Madison: University of Wisconsin Press, 1973), 1:170–172.
11. Liss, *Isabel,* 57–64; Payne, *History of Spain,* 1:171–172; Townsend Miller, *The Castles and the Crown, Spain: 1451–1555* (New York: Coward-McCann, Inc., 1963), 30–50.
12. Liss, *Isabel,* 65–67; Miller, *Castles,* 50–56; Irwin R. Blacker, ed., *Prescott's Histories: The Rise and Decline of the Spanish Empire* (New York: The Viking Press, 1963), 21–24.
13. Liss, *Isabel,* 67–75; Blacker, *Prescott,* 24–28.
14. Liss, *Isabel,* 65–80; Blacker, *Prescott,* 24–30; Miller, *Castles,* 56–63.
15. Liss, *Isabel,* 78–80; Blacker, *Prescott,* 25.
16. O'Callaghan, *History,* 657–669; Lomax, *Reconquest,* 167–178.
17. Payne, *History of Spain,* 1:77.
18. Thomas F. Glick, *From Muslim Fortress to Christian Castle: Social and Cultural Changes in Medieval Spain* (New York: Manchester University Press, 1995), 125–177.
19. Heath Dillard, *Daughters of the Reconquest: Women in Castilian Town Society, 1100–1300* (New York: Cambridge University Press, 1984), 12, 16.
20. Ibid., 26, 76, 78, 94.
21. Ibid., 98.
22. Ibid., 149–150.
23. Ibid., 156–161.

Chapter 2

1. Stanley G. Payne, *A History of Spain and Portugal,* 2 vols. (Madison: University of Wisconsin Press, 1973), 1:78–80.
2. Ibid., 1:80; Juan Beneyto Pérez, "The Science of Law in the Spain

of the Catholic Kings," in Roger Highfield, ed. *Spain in the Fifteenth Century, 1369–1516: Essays and Extracts by Historians of Spain,* translated by Frances M. López-Morillas (New York: Harper and Row, 1972), 290.
3. Evelyn S. Procter, *Alfonso X of Castile: Patron of Literature and Learning* (Oxford: The Clarendon Press, 1951), 64.
4. Ibid., 49–50.
5. Ibid., 51, 57–60; Payne, *History,* 1:80–81.
6. *Las Siete Partidas,* translation and notes by Samuel Parsons Scott (New York: Commerce Clearing House, 1931), xlix–lv; Procter, *Alfonso X,* 51.
7. A servivio a Dios
   La fé Católica
   Fizo nuestro Señor
   Onras señaladas
   Nascen entre
   Sesudamente
   Olvidanza
   From the introduction to each part of the *Partidas.*
8. Scott, *Partidas,* lviii–lix.
9. *Partidas,* Part 3, Title 18, Law 30; Part 2, Title 1, Law 2.
10. Ibid., Part 3, Title 7, Law 3.
11. Ibid., Part 3, Title 4, Law 3.
12. Ibid.
13. Ibid., Part 5, Title 12, Law 2; Part 5, Title 12, Law 3.
14. Ibid., Part 6, Title 16, Laws 4, 5; Part 4, Title 16, Law 2.
15. Ibid., Part 3, Title 16, Laws 1, 17.
16. Ibid., Part 3, Title 7, Law 6; Part 3, Title 23, Law 20.
17. Ibid., Part 7, Title 1, Law 2; Part 6, Title 18, Law 2.
18. Ibid., Part 6, Title 3, Law 5; Part 6, Title 16, Law 5.
19. Ibid., Part 7, Title 6, Laws 3, 4.
20. Ibid., Part 7, Title 33, Law 12; Part 6, Title 2, Law 2.
21. Ibid., Part 3, Title 18, Laws 58, 84, 85, 86.
22. Ibid., Part 4, Title 11, Laws 7, 17, 29; Part 3, Title 2, Law 5; Part 3, Title 18, Law 58.
23. Ibid., Part 1, Title 23, Law 12.
24. Ibid., Part 3, Title 29, Law 8.

25. Ibid., Part 5, Title 13, Law 34; Part 6, Title 13, Law 8.
26. Ibid., Part 5, Title 4, Law 10; Part 4, Title 12, Law 3.
27. Ibid., Part 5, Title 12, Law 36.
28. Ibid., Part 7, Title 9, Laws 8, 9, 18. To see how important the issue of honor was in colonial Latin America, see Lyman L. Johnson and Sonya Lipsett-Rivera's *The Face of Honor: Sex, Shame, and Violence in Colonial Latin America* (Albuquerque: University of New Mexico Press, 1998), Patricia Seed's *To Love, Honor, and Obey: Conflicts over Marriage Choice, 1574–1821* (Palo Alto, California: Stanford University Press, 1988), and Steve J. Stern's *The Secret History of Gender: Men, Women, and Power in Late Colonial Mexico* (Chapel Hill: University of North Carolina Press, 1995).
29. Ibid., Part 7, Title 14, Law 4; Part 3, Title 2, Law 5; Part 7, Title 17, Law 1.
30. Mari J. Matsuda, "The West and the Legal Status of Women: Explanations of Frontier Feminism," *Journal of the West* 24 (January 1985): 47–48.

Chapter 3

1. *Las Siete Partidas,* translation and notes by Samuel Parsons Scott (New York: Commerce Clearing House, 1931), Part 3, Title 2, Law 7; Part 6, Title 7, Law 5.
2. Ibid., Part 4, Title 1, Law 5; Part 4, Title 2, Laws 7, 15; Part 4, Title 3, Law 5.
3. Ibid., Part 5, Title 14, Laws 50, 51; Part 3, Title 2, Law 14.
4. Ibid., Part 4, Title 8, Laws 2, 3; Part 4, Title 9, Law 10.
5. Ibid., Part 4, Title 10, Law 2; Part 4, Title 9, Law 13; Part 7, Title 17, Law 1; Part 4, Title 9, Law 2; Part 4, Title 10, Law 6.
6. Ibid., Part 4, Title 13, Law 7.
7. Ibid., Part 4, Title 6, Law 16.
8. Ibid., Part 4, Title 6, Law 17.
9. Ibid., Part 3, Title 14, Law 9.
10. Ibid., Part 7, Title 7, Law 3; Part 4, Title 19, Law 3.
11. Ibid., Part 4, Title 12, Law 3.
12. Ibid., Part 4, Title 14, Law 2; Part 4, Title 13, Law 1.
13. Ibid., Part 4, Title 15, Laws 1, 3.
14. Ibid., Part 4, Title 15, Law 2. While canon law controlled the valid-

ity of marriage and is an important branch of law, it is not examined here because the topic is not the marriage itself but the property rights of women, which were controlled by the *Partidas* and various *fueros*.
15. Ibid., Part 4, Title 15, Law 5.
16. Ibid., Part 4, Title 15, Laws 4–8.
17. Ibid., Part 4, Title 16, Laws 1–3.
18. Ibid., Part 4, Title 16, Laws 4–6.
19. Ibid., Part 4, Title 16, Law 2.
20. Ibid., Part 7, Title 17, Law 13; Part 3, Title 14, Law 12.
21. Ibid., Part 4, Title 9, Law 2; Part 7, Title 17, Law 2.
22. Ibid., Part 7, Title 17, Law 15; Part 4, Title 10, Law 6.
23. Ibid., Part 7, Title 17, Laws 5, 7; Part 7, Title 22, Law 2; Part 7, Title 24, Laws 9, 25.
24. Ibid., Part 7, Title 9, Law 5; Part 5, Title 13, Law 53.
25. Ibid., Part 7, Title 8, Law 8; Part 7, Title 29, Law 5.
26. Ibid., Part 7, Title 8, Law 3; Part 7, Title 17, Law 14.
27. Ibid., Part 7, Title 20, Laws 1, 2.

Chapter 4

1. Townsend Miller, *The Castles and the Crown, Spain 1451–1555* (New York: Coward-McCann, Inc., 1963), 108; Juan Beneyto Pérez, "The Science of Law in the Spain of the Catholic Kings," in Roger Highfield, ed. *Spain in the Fifteenth Century, 1369–1516: Essays and Extracts by Historians of Spain*, translated by Frances M. López-Morillas (New York: Harper and Row, 1972); William H. Prescott, *History of the Reign of Ferdinand and Isabella, the Catholic, of Spain*, 2 vols. (London: George Routledge and Sons, 1867), 1:221–223.
2. Peggy K. Liss, *Mexico Under Spain, 1521–1556: Society and the Origins of Nationality* (Chicago: University of Chicago Press, 1975), 5, 8–10.
3. Ibid., 10, 12, 149; Prescott, *Reign of Ferdinand and Isabella*, 1:338.
4. C. H. Haring, *The Spanish Empire in America* (New York: Oxford University Press, 1947), 6–7.
5. Haring, *Spanish Empire*, 180–181; Stanley G. Payne, *A History of Spain and Portugal*, 2 vols. (Madison: University of Wisconsin Press, 1973), 1:205–206.

6. Haring, *Spanish Empire*, 182–184; Colin M. MacLachlan and Jaime E. Rodríguez O., *The Forging of the Cosmic Race: A Reinterpretation of Colonial Mexico* (Berkeley: University of California Press, 1980), 122–125.
7. Haring, *Spanish Empire*, 182–184; MacLachlan, *Forging*, 122–125 ; Jaime Suchlicki, *Mexico: From Montezuma to NAFTA, Chiapas, and Beyond* (Washington, DC: Brasseys, Inc., 1996), 31–33; Lesley Byrd Simpson, *Many Mexicos*, rev. 4th ed. (Los Angeles: University of California Press, 1966), 74–91.
8. Payne, *History*, 1:207–209; J. I. Israel, *Race, Class, and Politics in Colonial Mexico, 1610–1670* (New York: Oxford University Press, 1975), 125–131. The most complete and unbiased account of the Spanish Inquisition is Henry Kamen, *Inquisition and Society in Spain in the Sixteenth and Seventeenth Centuries* (Bloomington: University of Indiana Press, 1985).
9. Payne, *History*, 1:272, 285, 188; Prescott, *Reign of Ferdinand and Isabella*, 1:1, 13, 15.
10. Haring, *Spanish Empire*, 201–203; Payne, *History*, 1:209; Israel, *Race, Class, and Politics*, 125–131.
11. Haring, *Spanish Empire*, 179–208; Payne, *History*, 1:218–220.
12. Haring, *Spanish Empire*, 214; Payne, *History*, 1:274; Jaime Suchlicki, *Mexico*, 34–36; Liss, *Mexico Under Spain*, 48–68.
13. Haring, *Spanish Empire*, 242–244; Suchlicki, *Mexico*, 38–39.
14. Haring, *Spanish Empire*, 102–103; Payne, *History*, 1:255–256.
15. Haring, *Spanish Empire*, 103–107; Liss, *Mexico Under Spain*, 69–94.
16. Haring, *Spanish Empire*, 107–111; Liss, *Mexico Under Spain*, 48–68.
17. Haring, *Spanish Empire*, 110–115. For a detailed look at how the *Recopilación* came to exist, see Juan Manzano Manzano, *Historia de las Recopilaciones de Indias*, 2 vols. (Madrid: Ediciones Cultura Hispánica, 1950). The first volume recounts the preparation and work of Ovando, while the second volume deals mostly with the work of Pinelo and his followers.
18. *Recopilación de las Leyes de las Indias MDCCLXXXXI*, Book 9, Title 26, Laws 1–73, esp. Law 15 for converted Jews and Moors, Law 19 for Moors, Law 20 for Gypsies, Law 21 for mulattoes, Law 22 for married men having to take their wives, and Law 23 for single women not being allowed.

19. J. M. Ots Capdequi, *El Estado Español en las Indias*, 4th ed. (Mexico City: Fondo de Cultura Económica, 1965), 95–96, 98, 129.
20. *Recopilación*, Book 6, Title 10, Law 14; Book 6, Title 13, Law 9. See Lesley Byrd Simpson, *The Encomienda in New Spain: The Beginning of Spanish Mexico* (Berkeley: University of California Press, 1982) or John Francis Bannon, *Indian Labor in the Spanish Indies* (Lexington, Massachusetts: Heath, 1966).
21. *Recopilación*, Book 6, Title 13, Laws 14, 15.
22. Ibid., Book 4, Title 1, Laws 4–6; Book 6, Title 5, Law 19.
23. Ibid., Book 6, Title 11, Laws 1, 4, 15.
24. Ibid., Book 9, Title 26, Laws 24–30.
25. J. H. Elliott, *Imperial Spain: 1469–1716* (New York: St. Martin's Press, 1964), 157–161.
26. Ibid., 165–166; John Lynch, *Spain Under the Hapsburgs*, 2 vols. (New York: Oxford University Press, 1964) 1:180–181.
27. Richard Herr, *The Eighteenth-Century Revolution in Spain* (Princeton: Princeton University Press, 1967), 11–13; Haring, *Spanish Empire*, 8, 116, 139.

Chapter 5

1. Donald E. Chipman, *Spanish Texas, 1519–1821* (Austin: University of Texas Press, 1992), 101–113; Robert S. Weddle, *The French Thorn: Rival Explorers in the Spanish Sea, 1682–1762* (College Station: Texas A&M University Press, 1991), 192–207.
2. Chipman, *Spanish Texas*, 108–109.
3. Ibid., 105–113.
4. Mattie Alice Austin, "Municipal Government of San Fernando de Béxar," *Quarterly of the Texas State Historical Association* 8 (April 1905): 283–352; Carlos E. Castañeda, *Our Catholic Heritage in Texas, 1519–1936*, 7 vols. (Austin: Von Boeckmann-Jones Company, 1936–1958), 2:78; Jesús F. de la Teja, "Indians, Soldiers, and Canary Islanders: The Making of a Texas Frontier Community," *Locus: An Historical Journal of Regional Perspectives* 3 (Fall 1990): 84.
5. Jesús F. de la Teja, *San Antonio de Béxar: A Community on New Spain's Northern Frontier* (Albuquerque: University of New Mexico Press, 1995), 18; de la Teja, "Indians," 84–85, 90.

188   NOTES

6. Chipman, *Spanish Texas*, 127–129.
7. Austin, "Municipal Government," 285–288, 294; Castañeda, *Our Catholic Heritage*, 3:225–232; Chipman, *Spanish Texas*, 129–131.
8. Chipman, *Spanish Texas*, 135–137; de la Teja, *San Antonio*, 18–19.
9. Austin, "Municipal Government," 294–297; Castañeda, *Our Catholic Heritage*, 2:299.
10. Castañeda, *Our Catholic Heritage*, 2:301–304, 307–308; Chipman, *Spanish Texas*, 136–137; de la Teja, *San Antonio*, 47–48.
11. Castañeda, *Our Catholic Heritage*, 2:307–309; Chipman, *Spanish Texas*, 136–137.
12. *Recopilación de las Leyes de las Indias*, 1774 ed., Book 4, Title 5, Law 6; Book 4, Title 9, Law 13, cited in Austin, "Municipal Government," 300–305; Chipman, *Spanish Texas*, 137.
13. Chipman, *Spanish Texas*, 137–139.
14. Ibid., 139–140.
15. Ibid., 140–141.
16. Ibid., 145; de la Teja, "Indians," 87–91.
17. Chipman, *Spanish Texas*, 173–186.

Chapter 6

1. Carlos E. Castañeda, *Our Catholic Heritage in Texas, 1519–1936*, 7 vols. (Austin: Von Boeckmann-Jones, Co., 1936–1958) 3:90; Donald E. Chipman, *Spanish Texas, 1519–1821* (Austin: University of Texas Press, 1992), 139.
2. *Béxar Archives Translations (BAT)*, microfilm, 26 reels; reel 2, vol. 10, 95–99, 117–119, 169–174.
3. Ibid., reel 7, vol. 48, 76; Joseph W. McKnight, "Law Books on the Hispanic Frontier," *Journal of the West* 27 (April 1988): 74–84.
4. *BAT*, reel 2, vol. 10, 114–116; McKnight, "Law Books," 74–84.
5. *BAT* notes that this woman's real name was María Josepha Flores.
6. Randolph B. Campbell, *An Empire for Slavery: The Peculiar Institution in Texas, 1821–1865* (Baton Rouge: Louisiana State University Press, 1989), 10–12; *BAT*, reel 2, vol. 10, 100–105.
7. *BAT*, reel 7, vol. 48, 86; reel 6, vol. 45, 85–108.
8. Ibid., reel 6, vol. 45, 108.
9. Ibid., reel 3, vol. 17, 1–6.

10. Ibid., reel 2, vol. 10, 198–201.
11. Ibid., reel 3, vol. 18, 153–156, 145–148, 68–71.
12. Ibid., reel 3, vol. 18, 72–77.
13. Ibid., reel 7, vol. 48, 16–23, 27, 32, 38–39, 65. The present-day spelling of their family name is Carvajal, but it is spelled Caravajal in the archives, so this spelling is used here.
14. Ibid., reel 7, vol. 50, 15–21.
15. Ibid., reel 7, vol. 48, 43, 49, 65.
16. Ibid., reel 7, vol. 48, 142–154.
17. Ibid., reel 2, vol. 7, 117–118.
18. Ibid., reel 2, vol. 7, 119–121. The outcome of this case is not recorded in the Béxar Archives.
19. Ibid., reel 7, vol. 48, 73–78. The outcome of this case is not recorded in the archives.
20. Ibid., reel 2, vol. 10, 51–55
21. Joseph W. McKnight, "Spanish Law for the Protection of the Surviving Spouse," *Anuario de Historia del Derecho Español*, tomo 57 (1987): 373–395.
22. *BAT,* reel 3, vol. 18, 104–111.
23. Ibid.
24. Ibid.
25. Ibid., reel 7, vol. 48, 74.
26. Ibid., reel 7, vol. 49, 101–103.
27. Ibid., reel 5, vol. 32, 74–75.
28. Ibid., reel 4, vol. 24, 174–175, 183.
29. Ibid., reel 7, vol. 52, 41–116.

Chapter 7

1. Bryce Lyon, *A Constitutional and Legal History of Medieval England* (New York: Harper and Row, 1960), 19–35.
2. Ibid., 36–43. For a complete discussion of the change in the image of the king, see Ernst H. Kantorowicz, *The King's Two Bodies: A Study in Medieval Political Theology* (Princeton, NJ: Princeton University Press, 1957).
3. Carl Stephenson, "Feudalism and Its Antecedents in England," *American Historical Review* 48 (1943): 254–259.
4. Lyon, *Constitutional and Legal History,* 40–41; Carl Stephenson and

Frederick George Marcham, ed. and trans., *Sources of English Constitutional History: A Selection of Documents from A.D. 600 to the Present* (New York: Harper and Brother's Publishers, 1937), 22.
5. Lyon, *Constitutional and Legal History*, 36–137; Stephenson and Marcham, *Sources*, 14.
6. Lyon, *Constitutional and Legal History*, 73–82; Stephenson and Marcham, *Sources*, 20–23.
7. Stephenson and Marcham, *Sources*, 13, 19, 23–24; Lyon, *Constitutional and Legal History*, 49, 80–82.
8. Lyon, *Constitutional and Legal History*, 83.
9. Ibid., 41, 91–93.
10. Ibid., 94–95.
11. Ibid., 95.
12. Ibid., 96.
13. Ibid., 116–137; R. C. van Caenegem, *The Birth of the English Common Law* (Cambridge, U.K.: Cambridge University Press, 1973), 1–28; John Hudson, *The Formation of the English Common Law: Law and Society in England from the Norman Conquest to the Magna Carta* (New York: Longman, 1996), 86–117.
14. Lyon, *Constitutional and Legal History*, 138–165.
15. Ibid., 228–243.
16. Ibid., 279–280.
17. Ibid., 288–304; van Caenegem, *Birth of the Common Law*, 29–61; Hudson, *Formation of the Common Law*, 144–154.
18. Lyon, *Constitutional and Legal History*, 370–390. Scutage was shield money, the money that a knight could pay his liege in order to be exempt from military service. Tallage was a payment by towns or boroughs to the king in return for his protection. Both of these were instituted by the Normans as traditional feudal levies. Carucage was a tax on land instituted in 1194 and 1198 to help finance Richard's campaigns. All these taxes are examples of reciprocal rights and responsibilities, where a person or community owed the king in return for his obligation to them.
19. Ibid., 333–334, 431–436.
20. John Hamilton Baker, *An Introduction to English Legal History* (London: Butterworths, 1971), 139–142.
21. Ibid., 144–150; Sir Frederick Pollock and Frederick William Mait-

land, *The History of English Law Before the Time of Edward I,* 2nd ed. (London; Cambridge University Press, 1968), 15–19; Lyon, *Constitutional and Legal History,* 633–34.
22. Lyon, *Constitutional and Legal History,* 463.
23. Ibid., 464–465.
24. Ibid., 613–640.
25. *The Biographical History of Sir William Blackstone and a Catalogue of Sir William Blackstone's Works* by a Gentleman of Lincoln's-Inn (London: published by the author, 1782; New York: Rothman Reprints, 1971), 1–16; Daniel J. Boorstin, *The Mysterious Science of the Law: An Essay on Blackstone's Commentaries* (Chicago: University of Chicago Press, 1996), xiii–xiv.
26. Boorstin, *Mysterious Science,* 1–5.
27. St. George Tucker, *Blackstone's Commentaries with Notes of Reference to the Constitution and Laws of the Federal Government of the United States and of the Commonwealth of Virginia,* 5 vols. (New Jersey: Rothman Reprints, Inc, 1969. First edition Philadelphia: William Birch Young & Abraham Small, 1803), 1: 378, 418–430.
28. Kathleen Elizabeth Lazarou, *Concealed Under Petticoats: Married Women's Property and the Law of Texas, 1840–1913* in Harold Hyman and Stuart Bruchey, eds., *American Legal and Constitutional History: A Garland Series of Outstanding Dissertations* (New York: Garland Publishing, Inc, 1989), 16–19; Tucker, *Blackstone* 1:443–445.
29. Tucker, *Blackstone,* 1:443–445.
30. Susan Staves, *Married Women's Separate Property in England, 1660–1833* (London: Harvard University Press, 1990), 1–10, 27–55.
31. Ibid., 228–230.
32. Marylynn Salmon, *Women and the Law of Property in Early America* (Chapel Hill: University of North Carolina Press, 1986), 9–10.
33. Natchez Trace Collection Provincial and Territorial Records, 1759–1813, Center for American History, University of Texas at Austin (hereafter cited as NTC), Claiborne Co., Dec. 17, 1781; Claiborne Co., February 3, 1812.
34. NTC, Jefferson Co., January 9, 1804.
35. Ibid., August 13, 1807; March 1, 1808.
36. NTC, Natchez, September 17, 1795.

Chapter 8

1. Archivo General de la Nación (Mexico), Center for American History, University of Texas at Austin; *The Laws of Texas 1822–1897*, compiled and arranged by H. P. N. Gammel, with an introduction by C. W. Raines, 10 vols. (Austin: Gammel Book Company, 1898). Vol. 1 includes among other legal enactments the *Colonization Law of 1823* and the *Constitution of 1824*, and all laws passed by the state legislature of Coahuila and Texas. None of the laws included in Gammel's work that were enacted before 1835 changed the legal status of women.
2. Eugene C. Barker, *Life of Stephen F. Austin, Founder of Texas: A Chapter in the Westward Movement of the Anglo-American People* (Austin: University of Texas Press, 1969), 17–19; David B. Gracy, II, *Moses Austin: His Life* (San Antonio: Trinity University Press, 1987), 53–94; Gregg Cantrell, *Stephen F. Austin: Empresario of Texas* (New Haven: Yale University Press, 1999), 15–42.
3. Barker, *Stephen F. Austin*, 3–13; Gracy, *Moses Austin*, 166, 170–171, 197; Cantrell, *Stephen F. Austin*, 57–60, 71–72.
4. Gracy, *Moses Austin*, 200–203; Barker, *Stephen F. Austin*, 24–25. Barker entertains the possibility, which never occurs to Gracy, that Stephen might have gotten the information from Bastrop. Gracy wondered how Stephen could have learned the story, as he never saw his father alive after the meeting, nor were any letters extant. Barker includes the possibility of Bastrop telling the younger Austin about the elder, but does not stress the point. Cantrell points out that Stephen F. Austin and the Baron de Bastrop had many amicable dealings with each other. Bastrop could have fabricated the story entirely, embellished what actually happened to make himself look like the hero, or told the exact truth. No evidence proves or disproves any aspect of the story. Cantrell, *Stephen F. Austin*, 84–86.
5. Barker, *Stephen F. Austin*, 29–32; Cantrell, *Stephen F. Austin*, 80–103.
6. Barker, *Stephen F. Austin*, 29–42; Cantrell, *Stephen F. Austin*, 98–100.
7. Barker, *Stephen F. Austin*, 80–118. Cantrell has a good account of Austin's stay in Mexico and his imprisonment there, on pages 104–131. Joseph W. McKnight, "Stephen F. Austin's Legalistic Concerns," *Southwestern Historical Quarterly* 89 (January 1986): 244.

NOTES   193

8. Stephen F. Austin, ed., *Translation of the Laws, Orders, and Contract of Colonization from January 1821, Up to This Time...* (San Felipe de Austin, 1829), 59–65; Joseph W. McKnight, "Lawbooks on the Hispanic Frontier," *Journal of the West* 27 (1988): 74–84; Joseph W. McKnight, "Law Without Lawyers on the Hispano-Mexican Frontier," *The West Texas Historical Association Yearbook* 66 (1990): 51–65; McKnight, "Stephen F. Austin," 244, 247–257.
9. Austin, *Translation of the Laws*, 60–65.
10. Ibid., 59–65; McKnight, "Stephen F. Austin," 247–257. McKnight suggests that Austin's urban upbringing was the cause for his not including the clause on stray animals in the original regulations.
11. See Charles R. Cutter, *The Legal Culture of Northern New Spain, 1700–1810* (Albuquerque: University of New Mexico Press, 1995) on the legal system's purpose of protecting and enhancing the community. Austin, *Translation of the Laws*, 59–65; Cantrell, *Stephen F. Austin*, 142–146, 176–177, 213–214.
12. Austin, *Translation of the Laws*, 59–65.
13. Gammel, *Laws of Texas*, 1:97–98.
14. Ibid., 1:99–106.
15. Deed from Kuykendal to Peyton is in the Austin County Clerks Office Colonial Archives, Spanish Deeds, vol. 1, 1825–1835; deed from Morton to Austin in Austin County Clerks Office, Index to Deeds, Book A.
16. See Randolph B. Campbell, *An Empire for Slavery: The Peculiar Institution in Texas, 1821–1865* (Baton Rouge: Louisiana State University Press, 1989). Chapter 1 explains the motives and numbers of Americans moving to Texas; Barker, *Stephen F. Austin*, 201–225; Cantrell, *Stephen F. Austin*, 160, 189–192, 203–204.
17. Hans W. Baade, "'Marriage by Bond' in Colonial Texas" *Cornell Law Review* 61 (November 1975): 1–83. For the purposes of this study, it is important to remember that while canon law controlled the validity of the marriage itself, property laws in Mexico were controlled by the traditional law of the *Partidas*. It was these property laws that were continued in Anglo Texas.
18. Marriage Bonds, Austin County, 1824–1835, microfilm.
19. Austin Papers, Thomas Barnett to Stephen Austin, June 15, 1831.
20. Marriage Bonds, Austin County; Ron Tyler, et al., eds. *New Handbook of Texas*, 6 vols. (Austin: The Texas State Historical Association,

1996), 4:880; Henry Smith, "Reminiscences of Henry Smith" *Texas Historical Association Quarterly* 14 (1910): 31.
21. Gammel, *Laws of Texas*, 1:1041, 1293–1294, 2:640.
22. Nacogdoches Archives (NA), Center for American History, University of Texas at Austin, December 9, 1829; NA, July 31, 1824; Seguín's response, August 8, 1824.
23. Ibid., September 7, 1829; Report of March term, 1826.
24. Ibid., September 20, 1826; September 23, 1826.
25. Ibid., April 17, 1827; January 20, 1828; February 16, 1828.
26. Ibid., September 1, 1826; September 24, 1828; October 2, 1828.
27. Ibid., September 24, 1835; October 3, 1835.
28. Eugene C. Barker, ed., "Minutes of the Ayuntamiento of San Felipe de Austin, 1828–1832," *Southwestern Historical Quarterly* 23 (April 1920): 75.
29. Ibid., 23 (October 1920): 149.
30. NA, July 7, 1832

Chapter 9

1. Rupert N. Richardson, Ernest Wallace, and Adrian Anderson, *Texas: The Lone Star State*, 5th ed. (Englewood Cliffs, NJ: Prentice Hall, 1988), 48–58; Archie P. McDonald, "Anglo-American Arrival in Texas," in Ben Procter and Archie P. McDonald, eds., *The Texas Heritage*, 3rd ed. (Wheeling, IL: Harlan Davidson, 1998), 18–23. Other factors for Mexico's encouragement of Anglo-American immigration included the need to pacify Texas Indians and the need to improve the economy.
2. Richardson, et al., *Texas*, 83; Gregg Cantrell, *Stephen F. Austin: Empresario of Texas* (New Haven: Yale University Press, 1999), 221–227.
3. Richardson, et al., *Texas*, 84; Cantrell, *Stephen F. Austin*, 224–225.
4. Richardson, et al., *Texas*, 84–87; Cantrell, *Stephen F. Austin*, 224–260.
5. Richardson, et al., *Texas*, 87; Cantrell, *Stephen F. Austin*, 262; Eugene C. Barker, *Life of Stephen F. Austin, Founder of Texas: A Chapter in the Westward Movement of the Anglo-American People* (Austin: University of Texas Press, 1969), 348–359
6. Richardson, et al., *Texas*, 84–109. For more complete treatment of

NOTES   195

the revolution, see Paul D. Lack, *The Texas Revolutionary Experience: A Political and Social History, 1835–1836* (College Station: Texas A&M University Press, 1992) and Stephen Hardin, *Texian Iliad: A Military History of the Texas Revolution, 1835-1836,* illustrated by Gary S. Zaboly (Austin: University of Texas Press, 1994).

7. Archie P. McDonald, "Texas Independence," in Procter and McDonald, *The Texas Heritage,* 30–37; Cantrell, *Stephen F. Austin,* 267–296; Michael C. Meyer and William L. Sherman, *The Course of Mexican History,* 5th ed. (New York: Oxford University Press, 1995), 326–328.

8. Richardson, et al., *Texas,* 117–119; Archie P. McDonald, "Texas on the Rise," in Donald W. Whisenhunt, ed., *Texas: A Sesquicentennial Celebration* (Austin: Eakin Press, 1984), 80–81; McDonald, "Texas Independence," 39; Sam Houston, "Houston's Official Report," in *Documents of Texas History* (Lubbock: Texas Technical College, 1960), 113–115.

9. *Documents of Texas History,* 91–93.

10. *The Laws of Texas 1822–1897,* compiled and arranged by H. P. N. Gammel, with an introduction by C. W. Raines, 10 vols. H. P. N. Gammel, ed., *Laws of Texas,* 1: 9–26. (Austin, Texas: Gammel Book Company, 1898) 1:1039.

11. Ibid., 1:9–26.

12. "President Houston's First Inaugural Address," in *Documents of Texas History,* 123–124; Richardson, et al., *Texas,* 127–128; McDonald, "Lone Star on the Rise," 85–87; Stanley Siegel, *A Political History of the Texas Republic, 1836–1845* (Austin: University of Texas Press, 1956), 43–55.

13. Gammel, *Laws of Texas,* 1:1074, 2:177; James D. Lynch, *The Bench and Bar of Texas* (St. Louis: Nixon-Jones Printing Co., 1885), 26–31; Kathleen Elizabeth Lazarou, *Concealed Under Petticoats: Married Women's Property and the Law of Texas, 1840–1913* in Harold Hyman and Stuart Bruchy, eds., *American Legal and Constitutional History: A Garland Series of Outstanding Dissertations* (New York: Garland Publishing, Inc., 1989), 52–54.

14. Lazarou, *Concealed,* 54–55; Gammel, *Laws of Texas,* 2:177.

15. Lazarou, *Concealed,* 57–58; Gammel, *Laws of Texas,* 2:608.

16. Gammel, *Laws of Texas,* 1:1445, 1515; 2:37, 114, 156, 640, 678, 1056, 1064, 1065, 1110.

17. Archie P. McDonald, *Hurrah for Texas: The Diary of Adolphus Sterne, 1838–1851* (Waco: Texian Press, 1969), 11, 29, 40, 44. The diaries of pioneer women do not mention legal privileges as these women were too busy keeping alive and raising their families on a hostile frontier to worry about legal fine points. Even prosperous women such as Jane Long who owned several town lots, acres of land in the country, slaves, horses, and a hotel during the Republic period, did not need to sue anyone to enforce her legal rights. People seem to have simply followed the Spanish practices here, because they made more sense. Ann Fears Crawford and Crystal Sasse Ragsdale, *Women in Texas: Their Lives, Their Experiences, Their Accomplishments* (Burnet, TX: Eakin Press, 1982), 8; *Wood v. Wheeler*, 7 Texas Reports 19–21 (1851); *Jones v. Taylor*, 7 Texas Reports, 267–247; William Ransom Hogan, *The Texas Republic: A Social and Economic History* (Austin: University of Texas Press, 1990), 246; Lazarou, *Concealed*, 54, 59, 64, 73; Gammel, *Laws of Texas* 2:1293, 1459.
18. June 15, 1836, Nacogdoches Archives, University of Texas at Austin. The outcome of this case is not contained in the archives.
19. Ibid., September 17, 1840; October 9, 1840.
20. Ibid., November 1, 1840.
21. Ibid., May 8, 1837; October 8, 1837; June 19, 1837; January 6, 1838; January 2, 1838.
22. Andrew Frost Muir, ed., *Texas in 1837, an Anonymous, Contemporary Narrative* (Austin: University of Texas Press, 1958), 216; Lynch, *The Bench and Bar of Texas*, 65–73; J. Wilmer Dallam, *A Digest of the Laws of Texas* (Baltimore: John D. Toy, 1845), 548–553.
23. Hogan, *The Texas Republic*, 97–98.
24. Ibid., 98–99.

Chapter 10

1. Archie P. McDonald, "Lone Star on the Rise," in Donald W. Whisenhunt, ed., *Texas: A Sesquicentennial Celebration* (Austin: Eakin Press, 1984), 89–90
2. Ibid., 90; Rupert N. Richardson, Ernest Wallace, and Adrian Anderson, *Texas: The Lone Star State*, 5th ed. (Englewood Cliffs, NJ: Prentice Hall, 1988), 148.

NOTES

3. *Debates of the Texas Convention* (Houston, 1846): 10–11; Richardson, *Texas*, 147–149; McDonald, "Lone Star," 90.
4. Richardson, *Texas*, 90–91; McDonald, "Lone Star," 149.
5. *Texas National Register* (Washington, Texas), April 24, 1845.
6. Ibid., July 24, 1845.
7. *Debates of the Texas Convention*, 453–462, quotes on 461.
8. Randolph B. Campbell, ed., *Texas History Documents* to accompany Henretta, Brownlee, Brody, Ware, and Johnson, *America's History*, vol. 1 to 1877, 3rd ed. (New York: Worth Publishers, 1997), 44.
9. *Debates of the Texas Convention*, 37–45.
10. Ibid., 53–55.
11. Ibid., 417–418.
12. Ibid., 419–426, quotes on 420 and 421.
13. Ibid., 505–508.
14. Ibid., 598–601.
15. Ibid., 595–598, quote on 597.
16. Constitution of the State of Texas of 1845, Title 7, Sections 19 and 20 in *The Laws of Texas 1822–1897* compiled and arranged by H. P. N. Gammel, with an introduction by C. W. Raines, 10 vols. (Austin: Gammel Book Company, 1898) 2:1275–1302, sections cited on 1293–1294.
17. Ibid., Title 7, Section 22; Richardson, et al., *Texas*, 149.
18. Gammel, *Laws of Texas*. Volume 2 contains all the laws passed by the first legislature of the state of Texas. See 2: 1359; 2: 1450; 2: 1400; 2: 1452.
19. Ibid., 2:1459.
20. Ibid., 2:1462.
21. Ibid., 2:1715.
22. Ibid., 3:130.
23. Ibid., 3:130–131.
24. Ibid., 3:242.
25. Ibid., 3:364.
26. Ibid., 3:474.
27. *H. C. McIntire v. Harriet C. Chappell*, 2 Texas Reports, 378.
28. *Mitchell & Mitchell v. Wright, Administratrix*, 4 Texas Reports, 283.
29. *Callahan v. Patterson and Patterson*, 4 Texas Reports, 61.
30. Ibid.

31. Ibid.
32. *Cartwright v. Hollis and Wife*, 5 *Texas Reports*, 153.
33. Ibid.
34. *Cartwright v. Hollis and Wife*, 5 *Texas Reports*, 153.
35. Ibid.
36. Ibid.
37. *Hollis and Wife v. Francois and Border*, 5 *Texas Reports*, 195.
38. Ibid.
39. *Edrington v. Mayfield and Wife*, 5 *Texas Reports*, 363, emphasis added.
40. *Blanchet v. Dugat and Another*, 5 *Texas Reports*, 507.
41. Ibid.

Conclusion

1. *Texas Family Code*, Sections 3.001, 3.002.

Select Bibliography

Archives

Archivo General de la Nación (Mexico). Typescripts in the Center for American History. University of Texas at Austin.
Austin Papers. Center for American History. University of Texas at Austin.
Austin [Texas] County Clerk's Office, Colonial Archives.
Austin [Texas] County Marriage Bonds. Microfilm.
Béxar Archives Translations. Microfilm.
Nacogdoches Archives. Center for American History. University of Texas at Austin.
Natchez Trace Collection Provincial and Territorial Records, 1759–1813. Center for American History. University of Texas at Austin.

Published Primary Sources

Dallam, J. Wilmer. *A Digest of the Laws of Texas.* Baltimore: John D. Toy, 1845.
Documents of Texas History. Lubbock: Texas Technical College, 1960.
Foote, Henry Stuart. *Texas and the Texans or Advance of the Anglo-Americans to the South-West: Original Narratives of Texas History and Adventure.* 2 vols. Philadelphia: Thomas, Cowperthwait & Co., 1841.
Las Siete Partidas. Translated and annotated by Samuel Parsons Scott. New York: Commerce Clearing House, 1931.

The Laws of Texas, 1822–1897. Compiled and arranged by H. P. N. Gammel, with an introduction by C. W. Raines. 10 vols. Austin: Gammel Book Company, 1898.

McDonald, Archie P., ed. *Hurrah for Texas: The Diary of Adolphus Sterne, 1838–1851.* Waco: Texian Press, 1969.

Muir, Andrew Frost, ed. *Texas in 1837, an Anonymous, Contemporary Narrative.* Austin: University of Texas Press, 1958. Originally published in the *Hesperian,* September 1838–April 1839.

Recopilación de las Leyes de las Indias MDCCLXXXXI. Madrid: Gráficas Ultra, s. a., 1943. Originally published as *Recopilación de Leyes de los Reynos de las Indias,* mandadas imprimir y publicar por la Magestad Católica del Rey don Carlos II. Nuestro Señor. 4. Impresión. Hecha de órden del Real y Supremo Consejo de las Indias. Madrid, La viuda de d. J. Ibarra, impresora, 1791.

Sources of English Constitutional History: A Selection of Documents from A.D. 600 to the Present. Edited and translated by Carl Stephenson and Frederick George Marcham. New York: Harper and Brother's Publishers, 1937.

Texas Supreme Court. *Cases Argued and Decided in the Supreme Court of the State of Texas.* Cited as *Texas Reports.* Vols. 1–10.

The Visigothic Code (Forum Juridicum). Translated and edited by S. P. Scott. Littleton, CO: Fred B. Rothman & Co., 1982.

Secondary Works

BOOKS

Anon. *The Biographical History of Sir William Blackstone and a Catalogue of Sir William Blackstone's Works* by a Gentleman of Lincoln's-Inn. London: Published by the Author, 1782.

Baker, John Hamilton. *An Introduction to English Legal History.* London: Butterworths, 1971.

Barker, Eugene C. *The Life of Stephen F. Austin, Founder of Texas: A Chapter in the Westward Movement of the Anglo-American People.* Austin: University of Texas Press, 1969.

Basch, Norma. *In the Eyes of the Law: Women, Marriage, and Property in Nineteenth-Century New York.* Ithaca, NY: Cornell University Press, 1982.

Blacker, Irwin R., ed. *Prescott's Histories: The Rise and Decline of the Spanish Empire*. New York: The Viking Press, 1963.

Boorstin, Daniel J. *The Mysterious Science of the Law: An Essay on Blackstone's Commentaries*. Chicago: University of Chicago Press, 1996.

Campbell, Randolph B. *An Empire for Slavery: The Peculiar Institution in Texas, 1821–1865*. Baton Rouge: Louisiana State University Press, 1989.

———. *Gone to Texas: A History of the Lone Star State*. New York: Oxford University Press, 2003.

Cantrell, Gregg. *Stephen F. Austin: Empresario of Texas*. New Haven: Yale University Press, 1999.

Capdequi, J. M. Ots. *El Estado Español en las Indias*. 4th ed. Mexico City: Fondo de Cultura Económica, 1965.

Castañeda, Carlos E. *Our Catholic Heritage in Texas, 1519–1936*. 7 vols. Austin: Von Boeckmann-Jones Company, 1936–1958.

Chipman, Donald E. *Spanish Texas, 1519–1821*. Austin: University of Texas Press, 1992.

Collins, Roger. *The Arab Conquest of Spain: 710–797*. New York: Basil Blackwell, 1989.

———. *Early Medieval Spain: Unity in Diversity, 400–1000*. New York: St. Martin's Press, 1983.

Crawford, Ann Fears, and Crystal Sasse Ragsdale. *Women in Texas: Their Lives, Their Experiences, Their Accomplishments*. Burnet, TX: Eakin Press, 1982.

Cutter, Charles R. *The Legal Culture of Northern New Spain, 1700–1810*. Albuquerque: University of New Mexico Press, 1995.

De la Teja, Jesús F. *San Antonio de Béxar: A Community on New Spain's Northern Frontier*. Albuquerque: University of New Mexico Press, 1995.

Dillard, Heath. *Daughters of the Reconquest: Women in Castilian Town Society*. New York: Cambridge University Press, 1984.

Elliott, J. H. *Imperial Spain: 1469–1716*. New York: St. Martin's Press, 1964.

Glick, Thomas F. *From Muslim Fortress to Christian Castle: Social and Cultural Changes in Medieval Spain*. New York: Manchester University Press, 1995.

Gracy, David B., II. *Moses Austin: His Life*. San Antonio: Trinity University Press, 1987.

Grossberg, Michael. *Governing the Hearth: Law and the Family in Nineteenth-Century America*. Chapel Hill: University of North Carolina Press, 1985.

Hardin, Stephen. *Texian Iliad: A Military History of the Texas Revolution, 1835–1836*. Illustrated by Gary S. Zaboly. Austin: University of Texas Press, 1994.

Haring, C. H. *The Spanish Empire in America*. New York: Oxford University Press, 1947.

Herr, Richard. *The Eighteenth-Century Revolution in Spain*. Princeton, NJ: Princeton University Press, 1967.

Highfield, Roger, ed. *Spain in the Fifteenth Century, 1369–1516: Essays and Extracts by Historians of Spain*. Translated by Frances M. López-Morillas. Oxford: The Clarendon Press, 1951.

Hillgarth, J. N. *The Spanish Kingdoms, 1250–1516*. 2 vols. Oxford: Clarendon Press, 1976.

Hoff, Joan. *Law, Gender, and Injustice: A Legal History of U.S. Women*. New York: New York University Press, 1991.

Hogan, William Ransom. *The Texas Republic: A Social and Economic History*. Austin: University of Texas Press, 1990.

Hudson, John. *The Formation of the English Common Law: Law and Society in England from the Norman Conquest to the Magna Carta*. New York: Longman, 1996.

Israel, J. I. *Race, Class, and Politics in Colonial Mexico, 1610–1671*. New York: Oxford University Press, 1975.

Kamen, Henry. *Inquisition and Society in Spain in the Sixteenth and Seventeenth Centuries*. Bloomington: University of Indiana Press, 1985.

Kantorowicz, Ernst H. *The King's Two Bodies: A Study in Medieval Political Theology*. Princeton, NJ: Princeton University Press, 1957.

Lack, Paul D. *The Texas Revolutionary Experience: A Political and Social History, 1835–1836*. College Station: Texas A&M University Press, 1992.

Lazarou, Kathleen Elizabeth. *Concealed Under Petticoats: Married Women's Property and the Law of Texas, 1840–1913* in the series *American Legal and Constitutional History: A Garland Series of Outstanding Dissertations*. Harold Hyman and Stuart Bruchey, eds. New York: Garland Publishing, Inc., 1989.

Liss, Peggy. *Isabel the Queen: Life and Times*. New York: Oxford University Press, 1992.

SELECT BIBLIOGRAPHY

―――. *Mexico Under Spain, 1521–1556: Society and the Origins of Nationality.* Chicago: University of Chicago Press, 1975.
Lomax, Derek W. *The Reconquest of Spain.* London: Longman, 1978.
Lynch, James D. *The Bench and Bar of Texas.* St. Louis: Nixon-Jones Printing Co., 1885.
Lynch, John. *Spain Under the Hapsburgs.* 2 vols. New York: Oxford University Press, 1964.
Lyon, Bryce. *A Constitutional and Legal History of Medieval England.* New York: Harper and Row, 1960.
Manzano Manzano, Juan. *Historia de las Recopilaciones de Indias.* 2 vols. Madrid: Ediciones Cultura Hispánica, 1950.
Miller, Townsend. *The Castles and the Crown: Spain, 1451–1555.* New York: Coward-McCann, Inc., 1963.
O'Callaghan, Joseph F. *A History of Medieval Spain.* Ithaca, NY: Cornell University Press, 1975.
Payne, Stanley G. *A History of Spain and Portugal.* 2 vols. Madison: University of Wisconsin Press, 1973.
Pollock, Sir Frederick, and Frederick William Maitland. *The History of English Law Before the Time of Edward I.* 2nd ed. Cambridge: Cambridge University Press, 1968.
Prescott, William H. *History of the Reign of Ferdinand and Isabella, the Catholic, of Spain.* 2 vols. London: George Routledge and Sons, 1867.
Procter, Ben, and Archie P. McDonald, eds. *The Texas Heritage.* 3rd ed. Wheeling, IL: Harlan Davidson, Inc., 1998.
Procter, Evelyn S. *Alfonso X of Castile: Patron of Literature and Learning.* Oxford: The Clarendon Press, 1951.
Richardson, Rupert N., Ernest Wallace, and Adrian Anderson. *Texas: The Lone Star State.* 5th ed. Englewood Cliffs, NJ: Prentice Hall, 1988.
Rodriguez O., Jaime E. *The Forging of the Cosmic Race: A Reinterpretation of Colonial Mexico.* Berkeley: University of California Press, 1980.
Salmon, Marylynn. *Women and the Law of Property in Early America.* Chapel Hill: University of North Carolina Press, 1986.
Shammas, Carole, Marylynn Salmon, and Michael Dahlin. *Inheritance in America from Colonial Times to the Present.* New Brunswick, NJ: Rutgers University Press, 1987.
Siegel, Stanley. *A Political History of the Texas Republic, 1836–1845.* Austin: University of Texas Press, 1956.

Simpson, Lesley Byrd. *Many Mexicos.* Rev. 4th ed. Los Angeles: University of California Press, 1966.

Staves, Susan. *Married Women's Separate Property in England, 1660–1833.* London: Harvard University Press, 1990.

Suchlicki, Jaime. *Mexico: From Montezuma to NAFTA, Chiapas, and Beyond.* Washington, DC: Brassey's, Inc., 1996.

Tucker, St. George. *Blackstone's Commentaries with Notes of Reference to the Constitution and Laws of the Federal Governments of the United States and of the Commonwealth of Virginia.* 5 vols. South Hackensack, NJ: Rothman Reprints, Inc., 1969. First edition, Philadelphia: William Birch Young & Abraham Small, 1803.

Tyler, Ron, et al., eds. *The New Handbook of Texas.* 6 vols. Austin: Texas State Historical Association, 1996.

Van Caenegem, R. C. *The Birth of the English Common Law.* Cambridge: Cambridge University Press, 1973.

Warbasse, Elizabeth Bowles. *The Changing Legal Rights of Married Women, 1800–1861.* New York: Garland, 1987.

Weddle, Robert S. *The French Thorn: Rival Explorers in the Spanish Sea, 1682–1762.* College Station: Texas A&M University Press, 1991.

Whisenhunt, Donald W., ed. *Texas: A Sesquicentennial Celebration.* Austin: Eakin Press, 1984.

ARTICLES

Austin, Mattie Alice. "Municipal Government of San Fernando de Béxar." *Quarterly of the Texas Historical Association* 8 (April 1905): 283–352.

Cannon, Kelly M. "Beyond the 'Black Hole'—A Historical Perspective on Understanding the Non-Legislative History of Washington Community Property Law." *Gonzaga Law Review* 39 (2003-2004): 7.

Cloyd, Frances Spears. "Facets of Texas Legal History." *SMU Law Review* 1653 (Fall 1993): 52. Cornyn, John. "The Roots of the Texas Constitution: Settlement to Statehood." *Texas Tech Law Review* 1089 (1995): 26.

De la Teja, Jesús F. "Indians, Soldiers, and Canary Islanders: The Making of a Texas Frontier Community." *Locus: An Historical Journal of Regional Perspectives* 3 (Fall 1990): 84.

Graham, Kathy T. "The Uniform Marital Property Act: A Solution for Common Law Systems?" *South Dakota Law Review* 455 (2003): 48.

Kessler-Harris, Alice. "Taxing Women: Thoughts on a Gendered Economy: Symposium: A Historical Outlook: 'A Principle of Law but Not

of Justice': Men, Women, and Taxes in the United States, 1913–1948." *Southern California Review of Law and Women's Studies* 331 (Spring 1997): 6.
Matsuda, Mari J. "The West and the Legal Status of Women: Explanations of Frontier Feminism." *Journal of the West* 24 (January 1985): 47–48.
McKnight, Joseph W. "Law Books on the Hispanic Frontier." *Journal of the West* 27 (April 1988): 74–84.
———. "Law Without Lawyers on the Hispano-Mexican Frontier." *The West Texas Historical Association Yearbook* 66 (1990): 51–65.
———. "Spanish Law for the Protection of the Surviving Spouse." *Anuario de Historia del Derecho Español* 57 (1987): 373–395.
Paulsen, James W. "Community Property and the Early American Women's Rights Movement: The Texas Connection." *Idaho Law Review* 641: 32.
Ranney, Joseph A. "Anglicans, Merchants, and Feminists: A Comparative Study of the Evolution of Married Women's Rights in Virginia, New York, and Wisconsin." *William and Mary Journal of Women and the Law* 493 (Spring 2000): 6.
Rivers, Theodore John. "Widows' Rights in Anglo-Saxon Law." *American Journal of Legal History* 19 (1975): 208.
Saunders, Myra K. "California Legal History: A Review of Spanish and Mexican Legal Institutions." *Law Library Journal* 487 (Summer 1995): 87.
———. "California Legal History: The California Constitution of 1849." *Law Library Journal* 447 (Summer 1998): 90.
Stephenson, Carl. "Feudalism and Its Antecedents in England." *American Historical Review* 48 (1943): 245–265.
Zaher, Claudia. "When a Woman's Marital Status Determined Her Legal Status: A Research Guide on the Common Law Doctrine of Coverture." *Law Library Journal* 459 (Summer 2002): 94.

Index

Abd al-Rahman III, 176
abolitionists, 148, 149
abortion, 41–42
de Abrego, Francisco Flores, 73
acequias (irrigation ditches), 67, 76
Act of January 20, 1840, 138, 139, 141
"An Act to Provide for the Registration of the Separate Property of Married Women," 156
Adams-Onís Treaty, 178
adoption, 22, 38–39, 139, 140, 160
adultery, marriage and, 24, 29, 33–34, 37, 39, 40–41, 42, 43
Alexander VI (pope), 49
Alfonso I (king), 175
Alfonso II (king), 176
Alfonso III (king), 3–4
Alfonso IX (king), 176
Alfonso of Castile (king), 7–8
Alfonso of Portugal (king), 8
Alfonso V (king), 176
Alfonso VII (king), 176
Alfonso VIII, 176
Alfonso X (king), 6, 177
   reorganization of Castile's laws and, 15–18

Alfred (king), 93
alguacil (sheriff), 113, 115
Almansur, 176
de Almazán, Juan Antonio Pérez, 67
Alvarez de Pineda, Alonso, 63
Amador, Vicente, 78
American Southwest, 58
Anahuac, 134
Andrés, 84
Angevins, 95
Anglo-American Law, 137
Anglo-American settlers, Mexican Texas and application of Spanish/English laws to, 109–131
Anglo-Saxons
   British Isles and, *88*
   early, 87–89
   English history and, 87–94, 95, 96
   societal laws for, 89–92
de Angulo, Juan, 73
annexation, Texas' joint resolution for, 148–150
annulments, 33
Apaches, 68, 70
Aragon, 4, 5, 6, 7, 15, 45, 176
Armstrong, John, 153
de Arocha, Francisco, 68

INDEX

de Arredondo, Joaquín, 111
Arte de la lengua castellana, 46
Asturia, 3
audiencias (courts), 60
Augustinians, 50
Austin, Henry, 118
Austin, Moses, Mexican Texas and, 110–111, 178
Austin Papers, 121
Austin, Stephen F., 110, 111, 112
 Mexican Texas and, 113–118, 121
de Austin, San Felipe, 135
Austin's Colony, Mexican Texas and, 109–131
ayuntamiento, 129, 130, 135

Bache, Richard, 150
Bank War of 1832, 143
banks/banking, Texas and, 149, 150
Barnett, Thomas, 121, 122
Barrón, Gertrudis, 85
de Bastrop (baron), 111
Baylor, R. E. B., 152, 153
Beltrán de la Cueva, 7
Béxar Archives, 71, 73, 74, 79, 81, 84
Birdsall, John, 143
Birney, James, 48
Black Legend, xii
Blackstone, William, 98, 100, 103, 107
Blackstone's Commentaries, 103
Blanchet v. Dugat and Another, 167
Bolton, Herbert Eugene, xii
Bonaparte, Joseph, 178
Bonaparte, Napoleon, 110
bonds, 114
Boneo y Morales, Justo, 74
Bourbons, 61
de Bracton, Henry, 97, 98
Bradburn, Juan Davis, 134, 135
brothels, 32
Brown, George William, 150
Bustamante, Anastacio, 135

Cabello, Domingo, 75
cabildo (city government), 67, 68, 75, 129
Calhoun, John C., 148
Callahan v. Patterson and Patterson, 161
Calpurnia, 20
Canary Islanders, 68, 69, 70, 72
Canary Islands, 66
canon law, xiv, 16, 47, 100
capital punishment, 116
Caravajal, Francisco, 77
Caravajal, María, 78
de Caravajal, Mateo, 77
Carrillo de Acuña, Alfonso (archbishop), 8
Carroll, Mark M., xiv
Cartwright v. Hollis and Wife, 164
Casa de Contratación (House of Trade), 52, 56, 57, 60, 177
 functions of, 53–54
case law, San Fernando de Béxar and women's status in, 71–85
Castile, 4, 5, 6, 7, 9, 34, 45, 46, 48, 49, 172, 176, 177
 reorganization of laws in, 15–19
Castilian Law, 46, 48
 development of Spain and, 1–14
 New Spain and transfer of, 45–61
Castleman, Nancy, 120, 121
de Castro, Marcos, 78
de Castro, Ygnacia, 78
Cavelier, René Robert, 63
censorship, 53
Centralists, 135
Chancery Courts, 102
Charlemagne, 175
Charles II (king), 178
Charles III (king), 178
Charles IV (king), 178
Charles V (king), 53, 54, 60, 177
Chipman, Donald E., xv
Christians, 11, 41, 45, 51, 53
 Spanish, 3, 4, 5, 12

de Cisneros, Jiménez (cardinal), 51
civic rights, 101
civil capacity, 57
Civil Code of Louisiana, 137
Civil Regulations, 113
Clay, Henry, 148
Collier, Harriet, 125, 140
Collier, John Finley, 140
Collier, Robert, 125, 126
Collinsworth, James, 143
Coltins, Charles, 105
Coltins, Sarah, 105
Columbus, Christopher, 46
Commentaries on the Laws of England (Blackstone), 101, 107
common law
    English, xi, xii, xiii, 100, 139
    marriage, 119
community property, xii, 138
    laws, 171
    rights, 57
compadrazgo (godfather relations), 70
Concerning the Laws and Customs of England (Bracton), 97
concubines, 36, 37
conjugal relations, 33
conquistadors, 49
Consejo Real de las Indies (Royal Council of the Indies), 53, 58
considerations (payment), 32
Constitution for the Republic of Texas, 137
Constitution of 1824, 109
contracts, 32
    women's ability to make, 19, 25
conversos, 50–51
Córdoba, Vincenta, 141
de Córdova, Pedro, 52
corporal punishment, 116
cortes (local council), 46
    function of, 5–6
    royal power v., 6
Council of Castile, 54

Council of the Indies, 54, 55, 57, 60, 66
Council of Trent, 119, 120
Counter-Reformation, 52
courts, xi
    equity, xiii
Courts of Chancery, 100
coverture, 101
creditors, 149
crime, 92
    liability for, 19–20
criminal actions, women's liability for, 20, 28–29
criminal cases, 84
Crownover, John, 120, 121
Crusades, 95
de la Cruz, Gertrudis, 82
Curbelo, Joseph Antonio, 80
Curbelo, Juan, 67
custody rights, 35, 79–80
Cutter, Charles, xiv

Darnell, Nicholas Henry, 151, 153
daughters, inheritance laws for sons and, 2
Davis, James, 152, 153
death penalty, 43, 44
Delgado, Domingo, 79
DeWitt, Green, 129
DeWitt's Colony, 129
Díaz de Montalvo, Alfonso, 46
dishonor, honor and family, 28, 31–32, 39, 58
district judges, 113
divine right, 95
divorce, 33, 40
domestic relations
    concubines and, 18, 36, 37
    women's legal rights in, 19, 25–27
Dominicans, 50
dotal property, 26
dowry, 21, 25, 81
    marriage contracts and, 32, 34, 41

INDEX

Edrington v. Mayfield and Wife, 166
Edward I (king), 97, 99
el sabioi, 15
emigrants, 53
empresario grants, 110
encomenderos, 54, 55, 56, 58
encomiendas, 54, 58, 59
English Common Law, xi, xii, xiii, 73, 141
    codification of, 97–103
    history's impact on development of, 87–107
    inheriting property under, 102–103, 104–105
    marital status and, 101–102, 103–104
    taxes and, 97
    widows and, 103
    women's rights under, 101–102, 104–106
English history
    Angevins and, 95–98
    Anglo-Saxons in, 87–94, 95, 96
    English Common Law's development impacted by, 87–107
    jury trials in, 96
    Normans in, 94–95
equity courts, xiii
    estate, 34
Ethlered the Redeless (king), 93
Everts, Gustavus A., 153

Falcones, José, 143
family, importance of, 83
family law
    marriage and, 31–43
    Las Siete Partidas (Seven Divisions of Law) and, 31–44
Federalists, 135
femme coverts/soles, 163
Ferdinand IV (king), 178
Ferdinand of Aragon (king), 10, 177
    marriage of, 6–7, 8, 9

"One Law" and, 45–50, 60
Fernández de Castro, María, 74
Fernando I (king), 176
Fernando III (king), 176
fetus, 42
filibusters, 134
fines, 92
Finley, Rebecca, 141
Flores y Valdés, Josepha, 73, 74, 77, 80
Flores y Valdés, Rosa (doña), 73
Forbes, Emilia Sophia, 143
Forum Judicum, 1
France, 5, 8, 64, 149, 178
Franciscans, 50, 64
Free Masons, 156
Fuero de las leyes, 177
Fuero Reals (Royal Laws), 6, 46, 47
fueros (codes of laws), 12, 16

Galen, 15
Galicia, 175
Garcia III, 176
de la Garza, Gertrudis, 76
de la Garza, Raphaela, 73, 80
de la Garza, Tomasa, 75
General Law of Colonization, 116
Gertrudis de la Peña, María, 74, 75
Gibel al Tariq. *See* Rock of Gibraltar
Gillespie, John, 140
Gillespie, Mary. *See* Nettle, Mary
González, Ygnacio, 76
governments, local, 5–6
Granada, 5, 10, 45, 176, 177
grand jury indictment, 96
guarantor. *See* surety
guardianship, 22, 24
Guerra, Cayetano, 84
Guerra, Juan Ignacio, 84
Guerra, Matías, 84
gypsies, 56, 57

H. C. McIntire v. Harriet C. Chappell, 160

Index

Hadrian's Wall, 87
Hapsburgs, 60, 61, 178
Heath, Polly, 106
Hemphill, John (chief justice), 143, 145
   women's legal rights and, 152, 153, 154, 160, 161, 162, 164, 165–167
Henry I (king), 94
Henry II (king), 95, 177
Henry III (king), 96, 97
Henry IV (king), 7, 8, 177
heretics, 50
hermandades (brotherhood associations), 6
Hernández, Andrés, 77
Hernández, Antonia Lusgardia, 79
Hernández, Francisco, 77
Hernández, Josepha, 77, 78
Hidalgo, Father Francisco, 63
Hidalgo, Miguel, 178
Hijos Dalgo, 67
Hogan, Caty, 125
Hollis and Wife v. Francois and Border, 165
Hollis, Elizabeth, 164, 166
Hollis, William, 164, 166
Holy Roman Empire, 60
homestead clause, 155
homestead provision, 147
Homesteads Ungovernable: Families, Sex, Race, and the Law in Frontier Texas, 1823–1860 (Carroll), xiv
honor, 58
   family dishonor and, 28, 31–32, 39
Houston, Sam, 137, 142, 143, 149

Iberian Peninsula, 2, 3, 4, 5, 17, 45, 50, 172, 175, 176
illegitimacy, inheritance laws and, 36–38, 84
immigrants, 134

immigration, 11
   laws, 123
Indians, rights of women, 58
"infamous," 24
inheritance laws
   Anglo-Saxon, 94
   legitimacy/illegitimacy and, 36–38
   rule of primogeniture and, 98–100
   sons/daughters and, 2
"Instructions and Regulations for the Alcaldes," 113
Isabella of Castile (queen), 177
   marriage of, 6, 7, 8, 9
   "One Law" and, 45–50, 52, 60

jacales, 71
Jack, Patrick, 135
Jackson, Andrew, 137, 150
Jaime I, 176
Jesuits, 50
Jews, 10, 41, 45, 50, 51, 57
John (king), 95–96
Jones, Anson, 144, 149, 156
Jones, Jeremiah, 105
Joseph, Francisco, 74
Juan II (king), 7
Juana of Portugal ("la Beltraneja"), 7, 177
jury trials, 96

Keeling, Judith, xv
Kelton, Oliver P., 159
Kelton, Sarah Ann, 159
"King Cotton," 118
Kuykendal, Elizabeth, 118

de La Salle, Sieur, 63
Lagrand E. O., 141
Lamar, Mirabeau B., 137, 144
land grants, 138
land holding systems, 1, 76. *See also latifundia*
land ownership, 142

San Fernando de Béxar and, 75–78
de Lara, Bernardo Gutiérrez, 134
larceny, 29
Las Navas de Tolosa, battle of, 5
last suits, 141
latifundia, 1
Law for Promoting Colonization, 117
Law of April 6, 1830, 136
law suits, 142
　civil wrong doings and, 19
　women's ability to sue/to be sued in, 19, 28–29, 78–79
Laws of Toro, 46
lawyers, 72
Leal Goraz, Juan, 67
Leal, Juan Jr., 67
Leal, Magdalena, 78
legal capacity, 20
legal presumptions, 25
The Legal Culture of Northern New Spain 1700–1810 (Cutter), xiv
legitimacy, inheritance laws and, 36–38, 84
Leofwine, 93
León, 5
de Léon Pinelo, Antonio, 55
Leovigild (king), 175
life estate, 84
limpieza de sangre (purity of blood), 53, 57
de Liñán, Francisco, 73
Lipscomb, Abner S., 161, 162
Lizardo, Joseph, 82
Lone Star State, 109
Long, James, 134
López, Alberto, 76
Louisiana, 64
Louisiana Purchase, 110, 178

Madison, James, 111
Magee, Augustus W., 134
Magna Carta, 96

Maldonado, Francisco, 73
Maldonado, Luis, 73
Maldonado, María, 73
Manifest Destiny, 148
Manso (bishop), 52
marital property laws, 172
maritime laws, 16
marriages, xiv, 1, 12, 13, 118. *See also* domestic relations
　adultery in, 24, 29, 33–34, 37, 39, 40–41, 42, 43
　annulments in, 33
　common-law, 119
　conjugal relations in, 33
　contracts/dowries in, 21, 25, 32, 34, 41, 81
　divorce, 33, 40
　inheriting/disinheriting in, 34–35, 36, 143
　Mexican Texas and, 119–124
　property rights in, 34, 43, 138
　second, 36
　Las Siete Partidas (Seven Divisions of Law) and, 31–44
　widows/widowers and, 22, 23–24, 25, 35, 36, 41, 42, 57, 59, 73, 76, 103, 106, 118
Married Women's Separate Property in England, 1660–1833 (Staves), 103
Martel, Charles, 3
Martínez, Antonio María, 110, 111
Matagorda Bay, 63
Matilda (queen), 95
McIntyre v. Chappell, 163
McKnight, Joseph W., xv
Melián, María, 81
Menchaca, Diego, 85
Mexican Independence, 111, 135
Mexican law, 137
　Anglo settlers' clash with, 133–136
Mexican Texas, *112*
　application of Spanish/English laws

to Anglo-American settlers in, 109–131
    Austin, Moses, and, 110–111
    Austin, Stephen F., and, 110, 111, 112, 113–118, 121
    marriages in, 119–124
Mexico City, 64
Mineles del Padilla, Polonia, 142
Mission San Antonio de Valero, 64
Mississippi River, 178
Missouri Territory, 110
Mitchell & Mitchell v. Wright, Administratrix, 161
Moors, 3, 12, 41, 45, 57
Morton, Louisa Ann, 118
Muhammad I, 4
Muldoon, Father Michael, 121, 122
Munson, Micajah, 127
murder, 41, 42
Murray, Martha, 106
Murray, William, 106
Muslims, 3, 4, 5, 10, 11, 16, 51, 175, 176
Múzqui, Quiteria, 84

Nacogdoches, 127
Nacogdoches Archives, 124, 141, 142
Napoleonic Code, 137
Natchitoches, 112
Native Americans, 144
"natural rights," 133, 134
Navarre, 3, 5, 15, 46, 176
Navarro, Angel, 75
Neese, Elizabeth, 158
Nestles, William, 142
Nettle, Mary, 140
New Spain, *48*, 72
    transfer of Castilian Laws to, 45–61
de Nis, Manuel, 67
de Niza, Manuel, 77
Noaln, Philip, 134
Normans, 94–95

Núñez, Miguel, 79

oath helpers, 96
Odd Fellows, 156
Odom, Frances, 106
Old Three Hundred, 116, 118
de Oliva, María Eugenia, 74
"One Faith, One Crown, One Law," implementing, 45–61
Ordenamientos (laws and edicts), 46, 47
Ordenanzes Reales (Royal Ordinances), 46
de Ovando, Juan, 55
de Oyos, Juana, 77

Pacheco, Juan, 8
Padilla, Juan Antonio, 142
pagans, 51
Panic of 1837, 143
papal bulls, 50
paraphernal property, 26
pardons, 40
Pares, María Josefa, 143
Parry, Samuel M., 158
Patronato Real (Royal Patronage), 49, 54
Patterson, James D., 162
Patterson, Robert, 162
Patterson, Sarah E., 162
Pax Romana, 1
Pedro II, 176
Pelayo (king), 175
de la Peña, Sebastiana, 77
Pérez, Mateo, 82
Perry, Daniel, 118
Peyton, Jonathon C., 118
Philip II (king), 48, 52, 55, 60, 120, 177
Philip III (king), 177
Philip IV (king), 177
Philip V (king), 178
Pike, Zebulon, 134
"pin money," 103

214 INDEX

plaintiff, 106
de Plazas, Joseph, 73
Polk, James K., 147, 148
Polvaria, battle of, 4
Portugal, 3, 8, 46, 49
power of attorney, 72
   married women and, 73
   revocation of, 141
   siblings and, 73–74
   widows and, 73
Presidio San Antonio de Béxar, 64, 65
primogeniture, inheritance laws and rule of, 98–100
property
   community, 57, 138
   dotal, 26, 34
   inheriting, 102–103
   marital, 138
   paraphernal, 26, 34
   personal, 99–100
   protections of, 92
   real, 29
   separate, 156
   women's ability to hold, 19, 26–28, 139
property ownership laws, 2
property rights, xii, xiii, xiv, 2, 28, 29
   denial of, 2
   infringement of, xi
   loss of, 27
   women's, 143
property tax, personal, 97
Protestant Reformation, 52
Protestants, 53, 122
Provisional Government of Texas, 136
Ptolemy, 15
punishment, corporal/capital, 116
Pyrenees, 3

Quirk, Julianna, 124

Ramiro I (king), 176
Ramiro II (king), 176

Ramón, Diego, 76
rape, 2, 42, 93
Real Audiencias (Royal Courts), 56
Real Consejo de Indias, 177
real property, 29
reales (coins worth 1/8 peso), 81
Recared (king), 175
Reconquest *(Reconquista)*, 3, 4, 5, 6, 11, 13, 16, 57, 66, 69, 85, 99, 172, 177
   Spain at end of, *10*
   Spanish society's growth during, 12
Recopilación de las Leyes (Compilation of Laws), 55–56, 67, 72, 123
"red-backs," 144
regidor (councilman), 67
Republic of Texas, 147, 178
   Constitution for, 137
Republic of Texas Congress, 140
reputations, legal rights' correlation to good, 23–24
residencias, 55
Richard the Lion-Hearted (king), 95
Río Grande mission, 64
de los Ríos, Gabriel, 76
de Rivera y Villalón, Pedro (general), 65, 70
Roberts, John Finley. *See* Collier, John Finley
Roberts, John S., 140
Robertson, Stanley C., 140
Robinson, James W., 137
Rock of Gibraltar, 3
Roderic (king), 3
Rodrigo (king), 175
Rodríguez de Fonseca, Juan, 53
Rodríguez, María Eugencia, 79
Rodríguez, Salvador, 67
Rodríguez Tobar, Therés, 142
Roland, 175
Roman laws, 16, 18, 96
Romans, 1, 3
royal power, *cortes* v., 6

de Rubí (marqués), 70
Rumsey, Anna Maria, 106, 107
Rusk, Thomas Jefferson, 143, 150, 152, 153

Salmon, Marylynn, xiii, 104
Salvas, Antonio, 67
San Antonio, 65, 66, 67, 112
San Antonio de Béxar, 67, 111
San Antonio River, 64
San Fernando de Béxar, xi, 56, 68, 70
    case law and women's status in, 71–85
    description/living conditions in, 71
San Jacinto, battle of, 136
San Juan Bautista, 64
San Pedro Creek, 64
Sancho III (king), 176
Sancho VIII (king), 176
de Santa Anna, Antonio López, 135, 136
Saucedo, José Antonio, 116
Saucedo, Martín, 76
Scott v. Maynard, 143
second marriages, 36
seduction, 41
Seguín, Juan, 124
separate acknowledgments, 142
separate averment, 139
separate property, 26
Seville, 53
siblings, power of attorney and, 73–74
Sicily, 6
Las Siete Partidas (Seven Divisions of Law), xiv, 45, 46, 47, 56, 57, 61, 72, 85, 137, 177
    family law, 31–44
    history and components of, 15–30
    women's legal limitations/exceptions according to, 20–28
    women's legal status according to, 19–30
    women's loss of legal rights and, 23–24
Sixtus IV (pope), 50
slaves, 21, 23, 38, 39, 74, 135, 138, 141, 149, 154, 157, 158, 159, 163, 165, 166, 167
    limited rights of, 74–75
Smith, Henry, 140
sons, inheritance laws for daughters and, 2
Sosa, Juliana, 142
de Sosa, Juan, 85
Southwest, xii
Spain, 3, 5, 45, 47, 48, 49, 53, 178
    Castilian Law and development of, 1–14
    Reconquest and, *10*
Spanish Armada, 177
Spanish Borderlands, xii, xiv
Spanish Inquisition, 50, 51, 52
Spanish Laws, 139, 141
    Anglo-American settlers and application of English and, 109–131
Spencer, Nancy, 122
de St. Denis, Louis Juchereau, 63
Staves, Susan, 103, 104
Stephen (king), 95
Sterne, Adolphus, 140, 142, 143
succession, 136
surety, 21

Tariq ibn Ziyad, 3, 175
Tate, James, 126
taxes, 13, 49, 117
    English common law and, 97
Tejas Indians, 63
testimony, 20
Texas, xi, xii, xiii, xiv, 39
    banks/banking in, 149, 150
    Constitution for Republic of, 137
    constitution of 1845, 179
    creation of legal system and Republic of, 133–145

joint resolution for annexation of, 148–150
legal system in state of, 147–169
Provisional Government of, 136
Republic of, 178
Spanish legal system's arrival in, 63–70
Spanish/English laws and application to Anglo-American settlers in Mexican, 109–131
Texas Family Code of 1964, 171
Texas National Register, 149
Thomas Calvit v. Philip Alston, 106
Thorne, Frost, 142
Toledo, 8, 15, 176
torts, 28
Tours, battle of, 3
Towns, Sophia, 142
Trajan (king), 175
Travis, William Barret, 135
Treaty of Paris, 178
Treaty of Tordesillas, 49
Treviño, Juana Francisca, 73
true bill, 125
Truly, Elizabeth, 106
Truly, James, 106
trusts, 103
Tucker, St. George, 103
Tyler, John, 148, 149

de Urrutia, José, 68, 73
de Urrutia, Juana, 76
de Urrutia, Thoribio, 77

de Vaca, Cabeza, 63
vagabonds, 56
varas (33-1/3 inches), 67, 76
vassalage, 98
vecina agregada, 75
venire (court summons), 125
Villa de Béxar, 64
Villegas, Juan Joseph, 76
Vince, Allen, 140

Visigothic Code, 1, 16
Visigoths, 1, 3
visitadores, 55

Walker, Hiram, 141
Walker, Nancy, 141
War of 1812, 110
Wellborn, Matilda, 140
wergeld, 90
West, George, 140
West, Mary, 140
Whigs, 148
widows, 22, 23–24, 25, 76, 106, 118
    dower rights of, 103
    English Common Law and, 103
    power of attorney and, 73
    widowers and, 35, 36, 41, 42, 57, 59
Wilfredo the Hairy, 176
William Rufus (king), 94
William the Conqueror, 94
wills, 22, 34, 38, 72, 81, 99, 106, 139
witnesses, 72, 106
women
    case law from San Fernando de Béxar and status of, 71–85
    contracts and, 19, 25
    criminal actions by and liability of, 20, 28–29
    differences in legal rights of Hispanic and British, xi, 29, 73, 83–84, 101–102, 103–104, 106, 139, 141, 142
    domestic relations and legal rights of, 19, 25–27, 152–167
    Las Siete Partidas (Seven Divisions of Law) and rights of, 19–30
    power of attorney and, 73–74
    property ownership and, 19, 26–28
    property rights of, 143, 156
    protections for, 27
    rights of Indian, 58

social order and, 12–14
to sue/to be sued, 19, 28–29, 78–79
widows, 22, 23–24, 25, 35, 36, 41, 42, 57, 59, 73, 76, 103, 106, 118
wives, 25–30

Women and the Law of Property in Early America (Salmon), xiii, 104
Wright, John D., 161
Wynflaed, 93

Zaragoza, 176

www.ingramcontent.com/pod-product-compliance
Lightning Source LLC
Chambersburg PA
CBHW032249150426
43195CB00008BA/377